# SWORDS AND SAMURAI

## PHILIP STEELE
## FIONA MACDONALD

southwater

This edition is published by Southwater

Southwater is an imprint of Anness Publishing Ltd
Hermes House, 88–89 Blackfriars Road
London SE1 8HA
tel. 020 7401 2077; fax 020 7633 9499
www.southwaterbooks.com; info@anness.com

UK agent: The Manning Partnership Ltd
tel. 01225 478444; fax 01225 478440;
sales@manning-partnership.co.uk

UK distributor: Grantham Book Services Ltd
tel. 01476 541080; fax 01476 541061;
orders@gbs.tbs-ltd.co.uk

North American agent/distributor:
National Book Network
tel. 301 459 3366; fax 301 429 5746;
www.nbnbooks.com

Australian agent/distributor: Pan Macmillan Australia
tel. 1300 135 113; fax 1300 135 103;
customer.service@macmillan.com.au

New Zealand agent/distributor: David Bateman Ltd
tel. (09) 415 7664; fax (09) 415 8892

Publisher: Joanna Lorenz
Managing Editor: Helen Sudell
Editor: Joy Wotton
Designers: Matthew Cook, Alison Walker,
 Sarah Williams
Illustration: Rob Ashby, Stuart Carter, Richard Hook,
 Shane Marsh
Photography: John Freeman

Anness Publishing would like to thank the following
children for modelling for this book: Sarah Bone,
Lucilla Braune, Aileen Greiner, Otis Harrington,
Rachel Herbert, Francesca Hill, Alex Lindblom-Smith,
Sophie Lindblom-Smith, Daniel Ofori, Vanessa Ofori,
Edward Parker, Joshua Parris-Eugene, Claudia Martins
Silva, Levinia de Silva, Clleon Smith, Nicky Stafford,
Saif Uddowlla, Kirsty Wells, Tyrene Williams.
Gratitude also to their parents, and to Hampden
Gurney and Walnut Tree Walk Schools.

Previously published in two separate volumes, *Step
Into the Chinese Empire* and *Step Into Ancient Japan*

10 9 8 7 6 5 4 3 2 1

# CONTENTS

Introduction............................. 4

THE CHINESE EMPIRE........... 8
An Ancient Civilization............. 10
The Middle Kingdom............... 12
Makers of History..................... 14
The Sons of Heaven................... 16
Religions and Beliefs................. 18
Chinese Society......................... 20
Towns and Cities....................... 22
Houses and Gardens.................. 24
Family Life............................... 26
Farming and Crops................... 28
Fine Food................................. 30
Markets and Trade.................... 32
Medicine and Science................ 34
Feats of Engineering................. 36
Famous Inventions.................... 38

Workers of Metal.................... 40

Porcelain and Lacquer.............. 42

The Secret of Silk.................. 44

Dress and Ornament............... 46

Chinese Art.......................... 48

The Written Word................. 50

Musicians and Performers....... 52

Games and Pastimes............... 54

Travel by Land...................... 56

Junks and Sampans................. 58

Soldiers and Weapons.............. 60

Festivals and Customs.............. 62

ANCIENT JAPAN................ 64

The Land of the Rising Sun..... 66

Eastern Islands...................... 68

The Powerful and Famous....... 70

God-like Emperors................. 72

Nobles and Courtiers.............. 74

Shoguns and Civil Wars.......... 76

Samurai................................ 78

The Way of the Warrior.......... 80

Peasant Farmers..................... 82

Treasures from the Sea............ 84

Meals and Manners................. 86

Family Life .......................... 88

Houses and Homes.................. 90

The Castle Builders................. 92

Towns and Trade.................... 94

Palace Fashions...................... 96

Working Clothes ................... 98

The Decorative Arts.............. 100

Wood and Paper.................... 102

Writing and Drawing .......... 104

Poems, Letters and Novels .... 106

At the Theatre ................... 108

Travel and Transport ............ 110

Remote from the World.. 112

Gods and Spirits.......... 114

Monks and Priests ........ 116

Temples and Gardens...... 118

Festivals and Ceremonies.... 120

Glossary......................... 122

Index............................. 126

# Introduction

**BAMBOO BOOKS**
Over 3,000 years ago the Chinese wrote books on bamboo strips using ink made from plants and minerals.

THE LANDS AND PEOPLES of the Far East have always fascinated the rest of the world. In the Middle Ages, European merchants brought back tales of a vast and fabulous land they called Cathay. They spoke of a powerful emperor and his splendid palaces, of large cities, of marvellous temples and bridges. Lying beyond its shores, they said, were the beautiful islands of Cipangu, the Land of the Rising Sun, rich in gold and pearls. Today we know these two countries as China and Japan.

**PAINTING ON CHINA**
In the 1600s large quantities of pottery were exported from China and Japan to Europe. Scenes showing fish, flowers and daily life were especially popular.

## THE BIG COUNTRY

China is a huge country. Its present borders take in 9,597,000 square kilometres of eastern Asia. It is a land of crowded cities, of remote deserts and high mountain ranges, of wide plains crossed by great rivers. This is the most populous country on Earth, the home of 1,280.7 million people. Ninety-three per cent of these are Han Chinese, and the Chinese language is spoken by more people than any other in the world. China has over 50 other ethnic groups, speaking many languages and dialects.

**THE GOLDEN CASTLE**
Osaka Castle was built 400 years ago and is one of the tallest buildings in Japan. The five roofs were enriched with gold leaf.

**THE PALACE BUILDERS**
Throughout Japan and China, nobles and courtiers built fine palaces often with red-painted beams and spectacular curving roofs.

## ISLANDS IN THE EAST

In prehistoric times Japan was linked to the Asian mainland by bridges of land. These were flooded by rising sea levels about 20,000 years ago, creating the Sea of Japan and a chain of islands stretching north to south across a distance of over 2,400 kilometres. Japan has a land area of 369,700 square kilometres and a population of 127.4 million. Nearly all of its people are Japanese, although another ethnic group called the Ainu also live in the far north of Hokkaido island.

### SACRED LANDSCAPE
Mount Fuji in Japan has long been honoured as a holy place. Women were forbidden to go there until 1867.

### FESTIVAL FLOWERS
The flowering of plum blossom and cherry blossom heralded the Japanese festival of *Hanami.*

Modern Japan is a land of big, modern cities. However, the traditional landscape may still be seen too, with bays and small islands, fields of rice, volcanic mountain peaks, and flowering trees.

## EMPIRES AND WARRIORS

Both nations have very long histories and rich cultures. They have much in common, resulting from cultural exchange over thousands of years. Both the Chinese and Japanese founded ancient empires which lasted into modern times. Both had a long history of warfare and tried over the ages to gain control of the third country in the region, Korea. We know just what ancient Chinese soldiers looked like, for when Qin Shi Huangdi, first emperor of a united China, died in 210BC, his tomb was surrounded by a vast army of lifelike statues. These have been discovered and excavated. Japan's most famous warriors were the samurai, armoured knights who fought for noble families, mostly between 1185 and 1600.

### SAMURAI SWORDS
Japanese soldiers called the samurai took great pride in their weapons. They were skilled warriors from noble families and carried long swords called *tachi.*

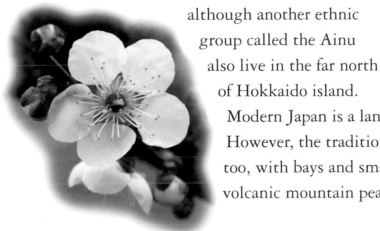

### TERRACOTTA WARRIORS
A lifesize army of soldiers and horses made of terracotta (baked clay) guards the tomb of Chinese Emperor Qin Shi Huangdi.

## WAYS OF LIFE

China, Korea and Japan all went through periods of being inward-looking and secretive, at times preferring to isolate themselves from outside influences such as foreign trade. At other times they were more open. In the Middle Ages, big fleets of Chinese ships explored the coasts of South-east Asia, Arabia and East Africa.

Chinese and Japanese farmers grew many of the same crops as each other, with rice as the most important everyday source of food. Tea was cultivated in both lands. Along the coasts, both peoples went to sea – as fishermen, or often as pirates.

### TRUTH AND HARMONY
Many people in China and Japan practised the teachings of the Buddha (the enlightened one).

The Chinese and Japanese both organized society into strict social ranks and classes. They were influenced by the Buddhist faith and also by the teachings of the Chinese philosopher Kong Fuzi (Confucius), who called for a well-ordered society based on family life, public service and respect for one's ancestors.

## SKILLS AND INVENTIONS

Both the Chinese and Japanese were skilled in technologies and crafts, producing shimmering silk textiles, impressive metalwork and pottery of the finest quality. In fact the earliest pottery known in the world was discovered in Japan. Many of the world's most important inventions originated in China, hundreds of years before they were adopted in other parts of the world – paper, printing, gunpowder, rockets, magnetic compasses, porcelain. The Chinese and Japanese excelled in painting and in calligraphy, the art of fine writing. About 1,200 years ago the Japanese based their new way of writing on the Chinese system.

### THE SECRET OF SILK
For years the Chinese tried to keep foreigners from finding out how silk was made.

### CHINESE VASE
The finest quality of pottery was known as porcelain. It was made with kaolin and baked at a very high temperature.

## PEOPLES DIVIDED

Despite these links, the Japanese and Chinese have always been very distinct from each other. Although both peoples live in eastern Asia, their languages are not related.

At various times in history, China and Japan were at war with each other. Between 1268 and 1281 the Mongol emperors who ruled China and Korea tried to become overlords of Japan. However, Japan was twice saved by storms which scattered the war fleets of these invaders. The longest and most bitter conflict between the two nations took place during the 19th century, when Japan invaded large areas of China.

**PLANTS TO ADMIRE**
The Japanese created beautiful gardens where they could enjoy gentle exercise, read or entertain friends and family.

**AT THE THEATRE**
Kabuki plays in ancient Japan were fast-moving, loud and very exciting.

## THE ISLES OF IMMORTALITY

An ancient legend about Qin Shi Huangdi tells how this first emperor of China wanted to live forever. He sent many ships across the ocean to search for the Isles of Immortality, where the people never died, staying forever young. The search was in vain. He finally sent the most famous magician in China to look for the islands. The magician never returned. Some say he settled in Japan, fearful of the emperor's anger. However, the emperor and the other great figures of the ancient Far East did achieve a kind of immortality, for their story lives on today.

## FINDING OUT

In this book we find out about the history of the Far East and the vital part played by its civilizations in world history. The ancient roots of modern China and Japan help us understand the way of life in those countries today. The same history also helps us understand modern western society, for Europeans and North Americans have looked to the Far East for inspiration in poetry, drama, art, design, architecture, philosophy and many other fields. Our journey of discovery is rich and colourful, as we discover the splendour of the Chinese imperial court, the trading caravans of the Silk Road, the castles of medieval Japan, lavish banquets, beautiful kites, lanterns and festivals.

**FLYING HIGH**
Kites were invented in China in about 400BC. Today kites and paper sculptures are an important part of any street festival.

# The Chinese Empire

The most ancient and influential civilization of the Far East grew up around two great rivers, the Huang He and the Chang Jiang, which wind eastwards from the high mountain ranges of Central Asia to the shores of the Yellow Sea and the East China Sea. This is China, land of the Great Wall and the Forbidden City, of rice fields and water buffalo, of emperors and mythical dragons, of jade and porcelain.

# An Ancient Civilization

IMAGINE YOU COULD travel back in time 5,000 years and visit the lands of the Far East. In northern China you would come across smoky settlements of small thatched huts. You might see villagers fishing in rivers, sowing millet or baking pottery. From these small beginnings, China developed into an amazing civilization. Its towns grew into huge cities, with palaces and temples. Many Chinese became great writers, thinkers, artists, builders and inventors. China was first united under the rule of a single emperor in 221BC, and continued to be ruled by emperors until 1912.

China today is a modern country. Its ancient past has to be pieced together by archaeologists and historians. They dig up ancient tombs and settlements, and study textiles, ancient books and pottery. Their job is made easier because historical records were kept. These provide much information about the long history of Chinese civilization.

**REST IN PEACE**
A demon is trodden into defeat by a guardian spirit. Statues like this were commonly put in tombs to protect the dead against evil spirits.

**ALL THE EMPEROR'S MEN**
A vast model army marches again. It was dug up by archaeologists in 1974, and is now on display near Xian. The lifesize figures are made of terracotta (baked clay). They were buried in 210BC near the tomb of Qin Shi Huangdi, the first emperor of all China. He believed that they would protect him from evil spirits after he died.

## TIMELINE 7000BC–110BC

Prehistoric remains of human ancestors dating back to 600,000BC have been found in China's Shaanxi province. The beginnings of Chinese civilization may be seen in the farming villages of the late Stone Age (8000BC–2500BC). As organized states grew up, the Chinese became skilled at warfare, working metals and making elaborate pottery and fine silk.

*c.*7000BC Bands of hunters and fishers roam freely around the river valleys of China. They use simple stone tools and weapons.

*Banpo hut*

*c.*3200BC Farming villages such as Banpo produce pottery in kilns. This way of life is called the Yangshao culture.

*c.*2100BC The start of a legendary 500-year period of rule, known as the XIA DYNASTY.

*c.*2000BC Black pottery is made by the people of the so-called Longshan culture.

*Shang bronze vessel*

*c.*1600BC Beginning of the SHANG DYNASTY. Bronze worked and silk produced. The first picture-writing is used (on bones for telling fortunes).

1122BC Zhou ruler Wu defeats Shang emperor. Wu becomes emperor of the WESTERN ZHOU DYNASTY.

*Zhou spearheads*

7000BC                 2100BC                 1600BC

## A HEAVENLY HALL

The Hall of Prayer for Good Harvests *(shown right)* is part of Tiantan, the Temple of Heavenly Peace in Beijing. It was originally built in 1420, but had to be rebuilt in the 1890s after it was destroyed by lightning. Buildings like these tell us about traditional technology and design, as well as about Chinese religious beliefs.

## THE HAN EMPIRE (206BC–AD220)

China grew rapidly during the Han dynasty. By AD2 it had expanded to take in North Korea, the southeast coast, the southwest as far as Vietnam and large areas of Central Asia. Northern borders were defended by the Great Wall, which was extended during Han rule.

## THE JADE PRINCE

In 1968, Chinese archaeologists excavated the tomb of Prince Liu Sheng. His remains were encased in a jade suit when he died in about 100BC. Over 2,400 pieces of this precious stone were joined with gold wire. It was believed that jade would preserve the body.

---

*Zhou soldier*

**771BC** Capital city moves from Anyang to Luoyang. Beginning of EASTERN ZHOU DYNASTY.

*c.*604BC Birth of the legendary Laozi, founder of Daoism.

**551BC** Teacher and philosopher Kong Fuzi (Confucius) born.

**513BC** Iron-working develops.

**453BC** Break-up of central rule. Small states fight each other for 200 years. Work begins on Grand Canal and Great Wall.

**221BC** China unites as a centralized empire under Zheng (Qin Shi Huangdi). Great Wall is extended.

**213BC** Qin Shi Huangdi burns all books that are not "practical".

*Chinese writing*

**210BC** Death of Qin Shi Huangdi. Terracotta army guards his tomb, near Chang'an (modern Xian).

**206BC** QIN DYNASTY overthrown. Beginnings of HAN DYNASTY as Xiang Yu and Liu Bang fight for control of the Han kingdom.

**202BC** The WESTERN HAN DYNASTY formally begins. It is led by the former official Liu Bang, who becomes emperor Gaozu.

**200BC** Chang'an becomes the capital city of the Chinese empire.

*terracotta warrior and horse*

**112BC** Trade with the peoples of Western Asia and Europe begins to flourish along the Silk Road.

780BC          550BC          210BC          140BC          110BC

# The Middle Kingdom

CHINA IS A VAST COUNTRY, about the size of Europe. Its fertile plains and river valleys are ringed by many deserts, mountains and oceans. The ancient Chinese named their land Zhongguo, the Middle Kingdom, and believed that it was at the centre of the civilized world. Most Chinese belong to a people called the Han, but the country is also inhabited by 50 or more different peoples, some of whom have played an important part in Chinese history. These groups include the Hui, Zhuang, Dai, Yao, Miao, Tibetans, Manchus and Mongols.

The very first Chinese civilizations grew up around the Huang He (Yellow River), where the fertile soil supported farming villages and then towns and cities. These became the centres of rival kingdoms. Between 1700BC and 256BC Chinese rule spread southwards to the Chang Jiang (Yangzi River), the great river of Central China. All of eastern China was united within a single empire for the first time during Qin rule (221–206BC).

The rulers of the Han dynasty (206BC–AD220) then expanded the empire southwards as far as Vietnam. The Chinese empire was now even larger than the Roman empire, dominating Central and Southeast Asia. The Mongols, from lands to the north of China, ruled the empire from 1279 to 1368. They were succeeded by the Ming dynasty, which was in turn overthown by the Manchu in 1644. In later centuries, China became inward-looking and unable to resist interference from Europe. The empire finally collapsed, with China declaring itself a republic in 1912.

## TIMELINE 110BC–AD960

AD9 The Western Han dynasty is challenged by Wang Mang.

AD25 The EASTERN HAN DYNASTY begins under Liu Xiu, after a peasant uprising. Its capital is at Luoyang.

*city of Luoyang*

c.AD26–225 Trade increases and a civil service is established. The first national library is built. Paper is invented, and an accurate calendar developed.

*book printed on bamboo*

AD65–100 The Buddhist religion takes root in China.

AD184 A peasant revolution called the Yellow Turban Rebellion takes place against Han dynasty rule.

AD220–280 Break-up of empire into separate kingdoms and dynasties. Cultural influence from India reaches China.

AD440 Daoism becomes official religion in north. Advances in mathematics and technology.

AD490 Longmen caves carved with Buddhist images.

AD581 SUI DYNASTY begins.

AD585 Main work on Grand Canal linking Chang Jiang with Huang He. Extension of Great Wall.

*Tao Yuanmin, Chinese poet c.AD300s*

AD618 Beginning of the TANG DYNASTY.

AD630–658 Chinese power and influence extends to cover Kashmir, Afghanistan and the river Oxus.

110BC      AD26      AD200      AD590

Mongol warrior

Caspian Sea

CENTRAL ASIA

MONGOLIA

Gobi Desert

The Great Wall

Beijing

Chang'an (Xian)

Grand Canal

Huang He

JAPAN

trader on Silk Road

Himalaya Mountains

Chang Jiang

Hangzhou

Chinese junk

Persian Gulf

River Ganges

rice

ARABIA

Arabian Sea

Bay of Bengal

INDIA

SOUTHEAST ASIA

South China Sea

flying fish

## TRADING EMPIRE

The map shows the extent of the Chinese empire during the Ming dynasty (1368–1644). Merchants transported luxury Chinese goods along the Silk Road, which stretched from Chang'an (Xian) to Mediterranean countries. Sea routes took traders to Vietnam, Korea and Japan.

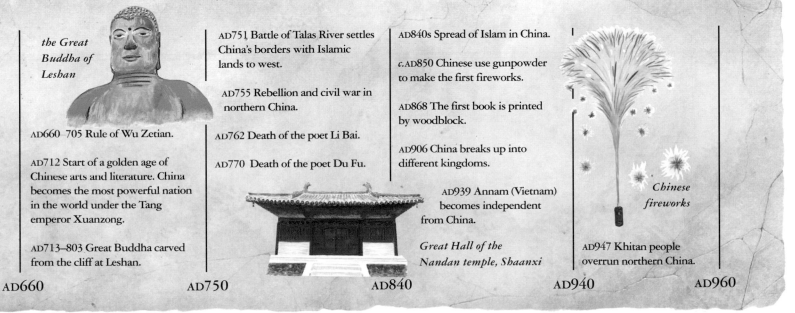

*the Great Buddha of Leshan*

AD660 705 Rule of Wu Zetian.

AD712 Start of a golden age of Chinese arts and literature. China becomes the most powerful nation in the world under the Tang emperor Xuanzong.

AD713–803 Great Buddha carved from the cliff at Leshan.

AD751 Battle of Talas River settles China's borders with Islamic lands to west.

AD755 Rebellion and civil war in northern China.

AD762 Death of the poet Li Bai.

AD770 Death of the poet Du Fu.

*Great Hall of the Nandan temple, Shaanxi*

AD840s Spread of Islam in China.

c.AD850 Chinese use gunpowder to make the first fireworks.

AD868 The first book is printed by woodblock.

AD906 China breaks up into different kingdoms.

AD939 Annam (Vietnam) becomes independent from China.

*Chinese fireworks*

AD947 Khitan people overrun northern China.

AD660          AD750          AD840          AD940          AD960

# Makers of History

Great empires are made by ordinary people as much as by their rulers. The Chinese empire could not have been built without the millions of peasants who planted crops, built defensive walls and dug canals. The names of these people are largely forgotten, except for those who led uprisings and revolts against their rulers. The inventors, thinkers, artists, poets and writers of imperial China are better known. They had a great effect on the society they lived in, and left behind ideas, works of art and inventions that still influence people today.

The royal court was made up of thousands of officials, artists, craftsmen and servants. Some had great political power. China's rulers came from many different backgrounds and peoples.

Many emperors were ruthless former warlords who were hungry for power. Others are remembered as scholars or artists. Some women also achieved great political influence, openly or from behind the scenes.

**LAOZI** (born *c.*604BC)
The legendary Laozi is said to have been a scholar who worked as a court librarian. It is thought that he wrote the book known as the *Daodejing*. He believed people should live in harmony with nature, and his ideas later formed the basis of Daoism.

**KONG FUZI** (551–479BC)
Kong Fuzi is better known in the West by the Latin version of his name, Confucius. He was a public official who became an influential teacher and thinker. His views on family life, society, and the treatment of others greatly influenced later generations.

## TIMELINE AD960–1912

*Kublai Khan*

AD960 The SONG DYNASTY begins.

1040 The Chinese invent a new method of printing that uses movable blocks of type.

1100 Further work is carried out on the Grand Canal.

1215–1223 Mongols led by Genghis Khan invade the north of China.

1260 Kublai Khan, son of the feared Mongol warrior and ruler Genghis Khan, becomes the Mongol emperor.

1275 Marco Polo said to have reached the Mongol capital of Khanbalik (Beijing).

*printed paper money*

1279 Mongols invade and conquer southern China, ending the Song reign. YUAN DYNASTY begins.

1340s Moroccan explorer Ibn Batuta visits China.

1349 Chinese settle at Singapore.

1351 Red Turban Rebellion against Mongol rule.

1363 Zhu Yuanzhang leads a fierce rebellion.

*Zheng He's rudder*

1368 Zhu Yuanzhang becomes emperor. Start of MING DYNASTY, with the capital at Nanjing.

1403–1435 Work on Great Wall.

AD960          AD1200          AD1278          AD1365

14

## QIN SHI HUANGDI (256–210BC)

Scholars plead for their lives before the first emperor. Zheng came to the throne of a state called Qin at the age of nine. He went on to rule all China and was given his full title, meaning First Emperor of Qin. His brutal methods included burying his opponents alive.

## HAN GAOZU (256–195BC)

In the Qin dynasty (221–206BC) Liu Bang was a minor public official in charge of a relay station for royal messengers. He watched as the centralized Qin empire fell apart. In 206BC he declared himself ruler of the Han kingdom. In 202BC he defeated his opponent, Xiang Yu, and founded the Han dynasty. As emperor Gaozu, he tried to unite China without using Qin's harsh methods.

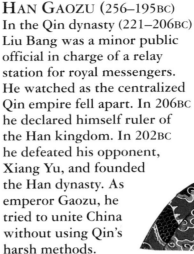

## EMPRESS WU ZETIAN
(AD624–705)

The emperor Tang Gaozong enraged officials when he replaced his legal wife with Wu, his concubine (secondary wife). After the emperor suffered a stroke in AD660, Wu took control of the country. In AD690 she became the only woman in history to declare herself empress of China.

## KUBLAI KHAN (AD1214–1294)

The Venetian explorer Marco Polo visits emperor Kublai Khan at Khanbalik (Beijing). Kublai Khan was a Mongol who conquered northern, and later southern, China.

1405–33 Chinese voyages of exploration under Zheng He.

1421 Beijing becomes the capital city of the Chinese empire.

*Manchu warrior*

1428 The Chinese are expelled from Annam (Vietnam).

1550 Japanese pirates mount raids on China. Mongols invade north again.

1644 Li Zicheng leads a rebellion against Ming rule. Manchu invasion. QING DYNASTY founded.

*Boxer rebels*

1673 Rebellions against Qing rule in south.

1839–42 First Opium War as Britain forces China to accept opium imports from India.

1842 Treaty of Nanjing. Britain gains Hong Kong.

1850–64 Taiping rebellion.

1858 Treaty of Tianjin. Chinese ports taken over by foreign powers.

1862 The Empress Dowager Cixi becomes regent.

1894–95 War with Japan. Loss of Taiwan.

1899–1900 Boxer Rebellion against Qing and foreign governments.

1908 Last emperor, Puyi, ascends to throne as a small boy.

1912 Declaration of republic by Sun Yatsen. Emperor Puyi abdicates.

*Puyi, the last emperor*

AD1405     AD1425     AD1650     AD1880     AD1912

# The Sons of Heaven

THE FIRST CHINESE RULERS lived about 4,000 years ago. This early dynasty (period of rule) was known as the Xia. We know little about the Xia rulers, because this period of Chinese history has become mixed up with ancient myths and legends. Excavations have told us more about the Shang dynasty rulers of over 3,000 years ago, who were waited on by slaves and had fabulous treasures.

During the next period of rule, the Zhou dynasty, an idea grew up that the Chinese rulers were Sons of Heaven, placed on the throne by the will of the gods. After China became a powerful, united empire in 221BC, this idea helped keep the emperors in power. Rule of the empire was passed down from father to son. Anyone who seized the throne by force had to show that the overthrown ruler had offended the gods. Earthquakes and natural disasters were often taken as signs of the gods' displeasure.

Chinese emperors were among the most powerful rulers in history. Emperors of China's last dynasty, the Qing (1644–1912), lived in luxurious palaces that were cut off from the world. When they travelled through the streets, the common people had to stay indoors.

### WHERE EMPERORS PRAYED
These beautifully decorated pillars can be seen inside the Hall of Prayer for Good Harvests at Tiantan in Beijing. An emperor was a religious leader as well as a political ruler, and would arrive here in a great procession each New Year. The evening would be spent praying to the gods for a plentiful harvest in the coming year.

### TO THE HOLY MOUNTAIN
This stele (inscribed stone) is located on the summit of China's holiest mountain, Taishan, in Shandong province. To the ancient Chinese, Taishan was the home of the gods. For over 2,000 years the emperors climbed the carved steps to the temple to offer prayers.

### IN THE FORBIDDEN CITY
The vast Imperial Palace in Beijing is best described as "a city within a city". It was built between 1407 and 1420 by hundreds of thousands of labourers under the command of Emperor Yongle. Behind its high, red walls and moats were 800 beautiful halls and temples, set amongst gardens, courtyards and bridges. No fewer than 24 emperors lived here in incredible luxury, set apart from their subjects. The Imperial Palace was also known as the Forbidden City, as ordinary Chinese people were not even allowed to approach its gates.

## "WE POSSESS ALL THINGS"

This was the message sent from Emperor Qianlong to the British King George III in 1793. Here the emperor is being presented with a gift of fine horses from the Kyrgyz people of Central Asia. By the late 1800s, Chinese rule took in Mongolia, Tibet and Central Asia. All kinds of fabulous gifts were sent to the emperor from every corner of the empire, as everyone wanted to win his favour.

## RITUALS AND CEREMONIES

During the Qing dynasty, an emperor's duties included many long ceremonies and official receptions. Here in Beijing's Forbidden City, a long carpet leads to the ruler's throne. Officials in silk robes line the steps and terraces, holding their banners and ceremonial umbrellas high. Courtiers kneel and bow before the emperor. Behaviour at the royal court was set out in the greatest detail. Rules decreed which kind of clothes could be worn and in which colours.

## CARRIED BY HAND

The first Chinese emperor, Qin Shi Huangdi, is carried to a monastery high in the mountains in the 200s BC. He rides in a litter (a type of chair) that is carried on his servants' shoulders. Emperors always travelled with a large following of guards and courtiers.

# Religions and Beliefs

"THREE TEACHINGS FLOW INTO ONE" is an old saying in China. The three teachings are Daoism, Confucianism and Buddhism. In China they gradually mingled together over the ages.

The first Chinese peoples believed in various gods and goddesses of nature, in spirits and demons. The spirit of nature and the flow of life inspired the writings which are said to be the work of Laozi (born *c.*604BC). His ideas formed the basis of the Daoist religion.

The teachings of Kong Fuzi (Confucius) come from the same period of history but they stress the importance of social order and respect for ancestors as a source of happiness. At this time another great religious teacher, the Buddha, was preaching in India. Within 500 years Buddhist teachings had reached China, and by the Tang dynasty (AD618–906) Buddhism was the most popular religion. Islam arrived at this time and won followers in the northwest. Christianity also came into China from Persia, but few Chinese were converted to this religion until the 1900s.

**THE MERCIFUL GODDESS**
Guanyin was the goddess of mercy and the bringer of children. She was a holy figure for all Chinese Buddhists.

**DAOISM – A RELIGION OF HARMONY**
A young boy is taught the Daoist belief in the harmony of nature. Daoists believe that the natural world is in a state of balance between two forces – yin and yang. Yin is dark, cool and feminine, while yang is light, hot and masculine. The two forces are combined in the black and white symbol on the scroll.

**PEACE THROUGH SOCIAL ORDER**
Kong Fuzi (Confucius) looks out on to an ordered world. He taught that the well-being of society depends on duty and respect. Children should obey their parents and wives should obey their husbands. The people should obey their rulers, and rulers should respect the gods. All of the emperors followed the teachings of Confucianism.

## FREEDOM FROM DESIRE

Chinese monks carved huge statues of the Buddha from rock. Some can be seen at the Mogao caves near Dunhuang, where temples were built as early as AD366. The Buddha taught that suffering is caused by our love of material things. Buddhists believe that we are born over and over again until we learn to conquer this desire.

## ISLAM IN CHINA

This is part of the Great Mosque in Xian (ancient Chang'an), built in the Chinese style. The mosque was founded in AD742, but most of the buildings in use today date from the Ming dynasty (1368–1644). Islam first took root in China in about AD700. Moslem traders from Central Asia brought with them the Koran, the holy book of Islam. It teaches that there is only one god, Allah, and that Muhammad is his prophet.

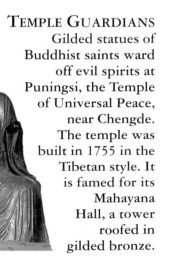

## TEMPLE GUARDIANS

Gilded statues of Buddhist saints ward off evil spirits at Puningsi, the Temple of Universal Peace, near Chengde. The temple was built in 1755 in the Tibetan style. It is famed for its Mahayana Hall, a tower roofed in gilded bronze.

# Chinese Society

THE RIVER VALLEYS AND COASTS of China have always been among the most crowded places on Earth. Confucius, with his love of social order, had taught that this vast society could be divided into four main groups. At the top were the nobles, the scholars and the landowners. Next came the farmers, including even the poorest peasants. These people were valued because they worked for the good of the whole nation, providing the vast amounts of food necessary to feed an ever-increasing population. In third place were skilled workers and craftsmen. In the lowest place of all were the merchants, because Confucius believed they worked for their own profit rather than for the good of the people as a whole. However, the way in which Chinese society rewarded these groups in practice did not fit the theory at all. Merchants ended up becoming the richest citizens, lending money to the upper classes. In contrast, the highly valued peasants often led a wretched life, losing their homes to floods and earthquakes or starving in years of famine.

## TOP BRASS
This is what important government officials would have looked like in the early 1600s. The government employed several thousand high-ranking officials. The civil service was regarded as the most honourable and best rewarded profession. The entry examinations were open to all men. Even the poor could rise to ruling class if they passed the examinations.

## THE IDEAL ORDER?
A government official tours the fields, where respectful peasants are happily at work. This painting shows an idealized view of the society proposed by Confucius. The district prospers and flourishes because everybody knows their place in society. The reality was very different – while Chinese officials led comfortable lives, most people were very poor and suffered great hardship. They toiled in the fields for little reward. Officials provided aid for the victims of famine or flood, but they never tackled the injustice of the social order. Peasant uprisings were common through much of Chinese history.

## WORKING IN THE CLAYPITS

The manufacture of pottery was one of imperial China's most important industries. There were state-owned factories as well as many smaller private workshops. The industry employed some very highly skilled workers, and also thousands of unskilled labourers whose job was to dig out the precious clay. They had to work very hard for little pay. Sometimes there were serious riots to demand better working conditions.

## DRAGON-BACKBONE MACHINE

Peasants enlist the aid of machinery to help work the rice fields. The life of a peasant was mostly made up of back-breaking toil. The relentless work was made slightly easier by some clever, labour-saving inventions. The square-pallet chain pump (*shown above*) was invented in about AD100. It was known as the dragon-backbone machine and was used to raise water to the flooded terraces where rice was grown. Men and women worked from dawn to dusk to supply food for the population.

## LIFE BEHIND A DESK

Country magistrates try to remember the works of Confucius during a tough public examination. A pass would provide them with a path to wealth and social success. A failure would mean disgrace. The Chinese civil service was founded in about 900BC. This painting dates from the Qing dynasty (1644–1912). There were exams for all ranks of officials and they were very hard. The classic writings had to be remembered by heart. Not surprisingly, candidates sometimes cheated!

## TOKENS OF WEALTH

Merchants may have had low social status, but they had riches beyond the dreams of peasants. They amassed wealth through money-lending and by exporting luxury goods, such as silk, spices and tea. The influence of the merchant class is reflected in the first bronze Chinese coins (*c.*250BC), which were shaped to look like knives, hoes and spades. Merchants commonly traded or bartered in these tools.

*knife*

*hoe*

# Towns and Cities

Cities grew up in northern China during the Shang dynasty (*c.*1600–1122bc). Zhengzhou was one of the first capitals, built in about 1600bc. Its city wall was seven kilometres long, but the city spilled out far beyond this border. Chinese cities increased in size over the centuries, and by the AD1500s the city of Beijing was the biggest in the world. Some great cities became centres of government, while smaller settlements served as market towns or manufacturing centres.

A typical Chinese city was surrounded by a wide moat and a high wall of packed earth. It was entered through a massive gatehouse set into the wall. The streets were filled with carts, beggars, craft workshops and street markets. Most people lived in small districts called wards that were closed off at night by locked gates. Temples and monasteries were a common sight, but royal palaces and the homes of rich families were hidden by high walls.

### The Sound of Bells
Bells were set up at temples and also on towers in the cities. They were struck at daybreak to mark the opening of the gates. Big drums were struck when they were closed at night.

### Chinese Skyscrapers
A pagoda (*shown far left*) soars above the skyline of a town in imperial China. Pagodas were graceful towers up to 15 storeys high, with eaves projecting at each level. Buildings rather like these were first seen in India, where they often marked holy Buddhist sites. The Chinese perfected the design, and many people believed that building pagodas spread good fortune over the surrounding land. Sometimes they were used as libraries, where scholars would study Buddhist scriptures.

### Make a Pagoda
*You will need: thick card, ruler, pencil, scissors, glue and brush, masking tape, corrugated card, 3cm x 1.5cm diameter dowel, embroidery bobbin, half a barbecue stick, paint (pink, terracotta and cream), thick and thin paintbrushes, water pot.*

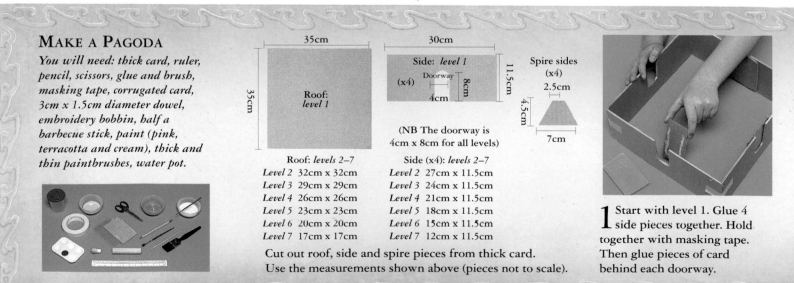

35cm

35cm

Roof: *level 1*

30cm

Side: *level 1*

(x4)  Doorway  8cm

4cm

11.5cm

Spire sides (x4)

2.5cm

4.5cm

7cm

(NB The doorway is 4cm x 8cm for all levels)

Roof: *levels 2–7*
Level 2  32cm x 32cm
Level 3  29cm x 29cm
Level 4  26cm x 26cm
Level 5  23cm x 23cm
Level 6  20cm x 20cm
Level 7  17cm x 17cm

Side (x4): *levels 2–7*
Level 2  27cm x 11.5cm
Level 3  24cm x 11.5cm
Level 4  21cm x 11.5cm
Level 5  18cm x 11.5cm
Level 6  15cm x 11.5cm
Level 7  12cm x 11.5cm

Cut out roof, side and spire pieces from thick card.
Use the measurements shown above (pieces not to scale).

1 Start with level 1. Glue 4 side pieces together. Hold together with masking tape. Then glue pieces of card behind each doorway.

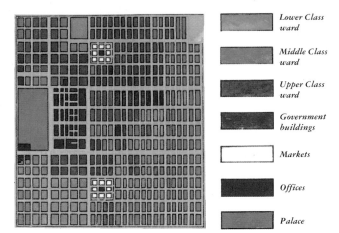

## CITY PLANNING

This grid shows the layout of Chang'an (Xian), the capital city of the empire during the Tang dynasty (AD618–906). The streets were grouped into small areas called wards. The design of many Chinese cities followed a similar pattern.

Lower Class ward

Middle Class ward

Upper Class ward

Government buildings

Markets

Offices

Palace

## WESTERN INFLUENCE

The flags of Western nations fly in the great southern port of Guangzhou (Canton) in about 1810. Foreign architectural styles also began to appear in some Chinese cities at this time. In the early 1800s, powerful Western countries competed to take over Chinese trade and force their policies upon the emperor.

## LIVING ON THE RIM

Cities around the edge of the empire were unlike those of typical Chinese towns. The mountain city of Lhasa is the capital of Tibet. It stretches out below its towering palace, the Potala. Tibet has had close political links with China since the AD600s. The country did remain independent for most of its history, but was invaded by China in the 1700s and again in 1950.

*Pagodas were built in China as early as AD523. Some of the first ones were built by Chinese monks who had seen Buddhist holy temples in India. Extra storeys were sometimes added on over the centuries.*

**2** Glue level 1 roof on top of level 1 walls. Allow to dry. Centre level 2 sides on roof below. Glue down and hold with tape. Add level 2 roof.

**3** Cut four 3cm wide corrugated card strips for each roof. The lengths need to match the roof measurements. Glue to edges of roof and sides.

**4** Assemble levels 3 to 7. Glue together spire pieces. Wedge dowel piece into the top. Stick barbecue stick on to bobbin. Then glue bobbin on to dowel.

**5** Glue spire on to top level. Use a thick brush to paint the base colour. Paint details, such as terracotta for the roof tiles, with a thin brush.

# Houses and Gardens

ALL BUILDINGS IN Chinese cities were designed to be in harmony with each other and with nature. The direction they faced, their layout and their proportions were all matters of great spiritual importance. Even the number of steps leading up to the entrance of the house was considered to be significant. House design in imperial China varied over time and between regions. In the hot and rainy south, courtyards tended to be covered for shade and shelter. In the drier climate of the north, courtyards were mostly open to the elements. Poor people in the countryside lived in simple, thatched huts. These were made from timber frames covered in mud plaster. They were often noisy, draughty and overcrowded. In contrast, the spacious homes of the wealthy were large, peaceful and well constructed. Many had beautiful gardens, filled with peonies, bamboo and wisteria. Some of these gardens also contained orchards, ponds and pavilions.

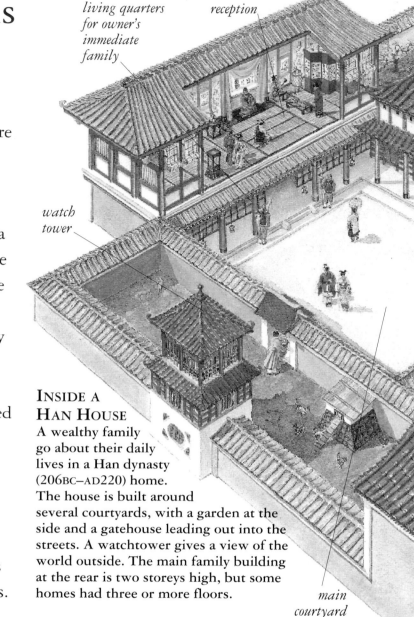

*living quarters for owner's immediate family*

*reception*

*watch tower*

*main courtyard*

### INSIDE A HAN HOUSE
A wealthy family go about their daily lives in a Han dynasty (206BC–AD220) home. The house is built around several courtyards, with a garden at the side and a gatehouse leading out into the streets. A watchtower gives a view of the world outside. The main family building at the rear is two storeys high, but some homes had three or more floors.

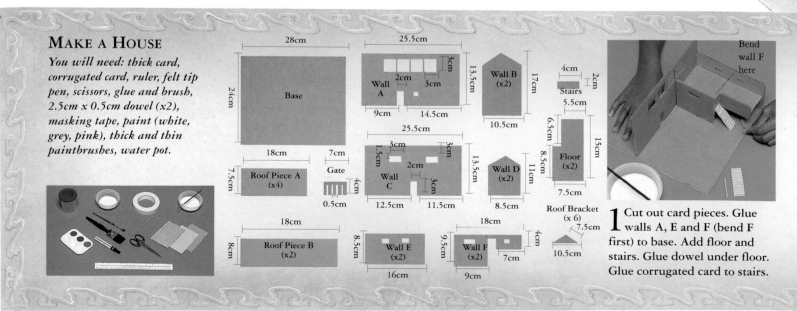

### MAKE A HOUSE
*You will need: thick card, corrugated card, ruler, felt tip pen, scissors, glue and brush, 2.5cm x 0.5cm dowel (x2), masking tape, paint (white, grey, pink), thick and thin paintbrushes, water pot.*

Base — 28cm × 24cm

Wall A — 25.5cm × 13.5cm; 3cm; 2cm; 3cm; 9cm; 14.5cm

Wall B (x2) — 13.5cm; 17cm; 10.5cm

Stairs — 4cm; 2cm; 5.5cm

Roof Piece A (x4) — 18cm × 7.5cm; Gate 7cm × 4cm; 0.5cm

Wall C — 25.5cm; 1.5cm; 3cm; 2cm; 3cm; 13.5cm; 12.5cm; 11.5cm

Wall D (x2) — 6.5cm; 8.5cm; 11cm; 8.5cm

Floor (x2) — 15cm; 7.5cm

Roof Piece B (x2) — 18cm × 8cm

Wall E (x2) — 8.5cm × 16cm

Wall F (x2) — 9.5cm; 4cm; 7cm; 9cm

Roof Bracket (x6) — 7.5cm; 10.5cm

Bend wall F here

1 Cut out card pieces. Glue walls A, E and F (bend F first) to base. Add floor and stairs. Glue dowel under floor. Glue corrugated card to stairs.

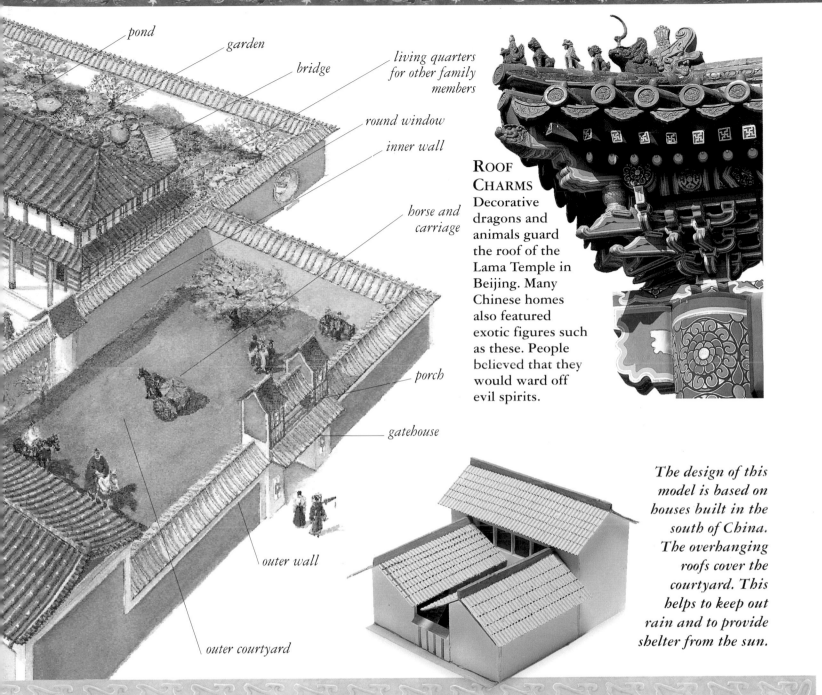

pond

garden

bridge

living quarters for other family members

round window

inner wall

horse and carriage

porch

gatehouse

outer wall

outer courtyard

**ROOF CHARMS**
Decorative dragons and animals guard the roof of the Lama Temple in Beijing. Many Chinese homes also featured exotic figures such as these. People believed that they would ward off evil spirits.

*The design of this model is based on houses built in the south of China. The overhanging roofs cover the courtyard. This helps to keep out rain and to provide shelter from the sun.*

**2** To assemble second side, repeat method described in step 1. If necessary, hold pieces together with masking tape while the glue dries.

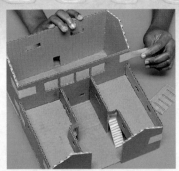

**3** Glue B walls to the sides of the base, C wall to the back and D walls to the front. Hold with tape while glue dries. Glue gate between D walls.

**4** Assemble A roofs (x2) and B roof (x1). Fix brackets underneath. Glue corrugated card (cut to same size as roof pieces) to top side of roofs.

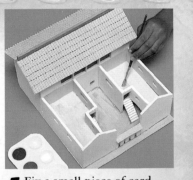

**5** Fix a small piece of card over the gate to make a porch. Paint house, as shown. Use a thin brush to create a tile effect on the removable roofs.

# Family Life

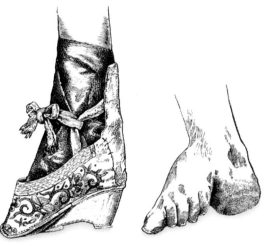

KONG FUZI (CONFUCIUS) taught that just as the emperor was head of the state, the oldest man was head of the household and should be obeyed by his family. In reality, his wife ran the home and often controlled the daily lives of the other women in the household.

During the Han dynasty (206BC–AD220) noblewomen were kept apart from the outside world. They could only gaze at the streets from the watchtowers of their homes. It was not until the Song dynasty (AD960–1279) that they gained more freedom. In poor households women worked all day, spending long, tiring hours farming, cooking, sweeping and washing.

For the children of poorer families, education meant learning to do the work their parents did. This involved carrying goods to market, or helping with the threshing or planting. The children of wealthier parents had private tutors at home. Boys hoping to become scholars or civil servants learned to read and write Chinese characters. They also studied maths and the works of Kong Fuzi.

### LESSONS FOR THE BOYS
A group of Chinese boys take their school lessons. In imperial China, boys generally received a more academic education than girls. Girls were mainly taught music, handicrafts, painting and social skills. Some girls were taught academic subjects, but they were not allowed to sit the civil service examinations.

### CHINESE MARRIAGE
A wedding ceremony takes place in the late 1800s. In imperial China, weddings were arranged by the parents of the bride and groom, rather than by the couples themselves. It was expected that the couple would respect their parents' wishes, even if they didn't like each other!

### FOOT BINDING
This foot looks elegant in its beautiful slipper, but it's a different story when the slipper is removed. Just when life was improving for Chinese women, the cruel new custom of footbinding was introduced. Dancers had bound their feet for some years in the belief that it made them look dainty. In the Song dynasty the custom spread to wealthy and noble families. Little girls of five or so had their feet bound up so tightly that they became terribly deformed.

## TAKING IT EASY

A noblewoman living during the Qing dynasty relaxes on a garden terrace with her children (*c.*1840). She is very fortunate as she has little else to do but enjoy the pleasant surroundings of her home. In rich families like hers, servants did most of the hard work, such as cooking, cleaning and washing. Wealthy Chinese families kept many servants, who usually lived in quarters inside their employer's home. Servants accounted for a large number of the workforce in imperial China. During the Ming dynasty (1368–1644), some 9,000 maidservants were employed at the imperial palace in Beijing alone!

## RESPECT AND HONOUR

Children in the 1100s bow respectfully to their parents. Confucius taught that people should value and honour their families, including their ancestors. He believed that this helped to create a more orderly and virtuous society.

## THE EMPEROR AND HIS MANY WIVES

Sui dynasty emperor Yangdi (AD581–618) rides out with his many womenfolk. Like many emperors, Yangdi was surrounded by women. An emperor married one woman, who would then become his empress, but he would still enjoy the company of concubines (secondary wives).

# Farming and Crops

EIGHT THOUSAND YEARS AGO most Chinese people were already living by farming. The best soil lay beside the great rivers in central and eastern China, where floods left behind rich, fertile mud. As today, wheat and millet were grown in the north. This region was mostly farmed by peasants with small plots of land. Rice was cultivated in the warm, wet south, where wealthy city-dwellers owned large estates. Pears and oranges were grown in orchards.

Tea, later to become one of China's most famous exports, was first cultivated about 1,700 years ago. Hemp was also grown for its fibres. During the 500s BC, cotton was introduced. Farmers raised pigs, ducks, chickens and geese, while oxen and water buffalo were used as labouring animals on the farm.

Most peasants used basic tools, such as stone hoes and wooden rakes. Ploughs with iron blades were used from about 600BC. Other inventions to help farmers were developed in the next few hundred years, including the wheelbarrow, a pedal hammer for husking grain and a rotary winnowing fan.

**PIGS ARE FARM FAVOURITES**
This pottery model of pigs in their sty dates back about 2,000 years. Pigs were popular farm animals, as they are easy to feed and most parts of a pig can be eaten. They were kept in the city as well as in rural country areas.

**FEEDING THE MANY**
Rice has been grown in the wetter regions of China since ancient times. Wheat and millet are grown in the drier regions. Sprouts of the Indian mung bean add important vitamins to many dishes.

*mung beans*

*millet*

*rice*

*wheat*

**CHINESE TEAS**
Delicate leaves of tea are picked from the bushes and gathered in large baskets on this estate in the 1800s. The Chinese cultivated tea in ancient times, but it became much more popular during the Tang dynasty (AD618–906). The leaves were picked, laid out in the sun, rolled by hand and then dried over charcoal fires.

## WORKING THE LAND

A farmer uses a pair of strong oxen to help him plough his land. This wall painting found in Jiayuguan dates back to about 100BC. Oxen saved farmers a lot of time and effort. The Chinese first used oxen in farming in about 1122BC.

## KEEPING WARM

This model of a Chinese farmer's lambing shed dates from about 100BC, during the Han dynasty. Sheepskins were worn for warmth, but wool never became an important textile for clothes or blankets in China.

## HARVESTING RICE – CHINA'S MAIN FOOD

Chinese peasants pull up rice plants for threshing and winnowing in the 1600s. Farming methods were passed on by word of mouth and in handbooks from the earliest times. They advised farmers on everything from fertilizing the soil to controlling pests.

## A TIMELESS SCENE

Peasants bend over to plant out rows of rice seedlings in the flooded paddy fields of Yunnan province, in southwest China. This modern photograph is a typical scene of agricultural life in China's warm and wet southwest region. Little has changed in hundreds of years of farming.

# Fine Food

CHINESE COOKS TODAY are among the best in the world, with skills gained over thousands of years. Rice was the basis of most meals in ancient China, especially in the south where it was grown. Northerners used wheat flour to make noodles and buns. Food varied greatly between the regions. The north was famous for pancakes, dumplings, lamb and duck dishes. In the west, Sichuan was renowned for its hot chilli peppers. Mushrooms and bamboo shoots were popular along the lower Chang Jiang (Yangzi River).

For many people, meat was a rare treat. It included chicken, pork and many kinds of fish, and was often spiced with garlic and ginger. Dishes featured meat that people from other parts of the world might find strange, such as turtle, dog, monkey and bear. Food was stewed, steamed or fried. The use of chopsticks and bowls dates back to the Shang dynasty (c.1600–1122BC).

**THE KITCHEN GOD**
In every kitchen hung a paper picture of the kitchen god and his wife. Each year, on the 24th day of the 12th month, sweets were put out as offerings. Then the picture was taken down and burned. A new one was put in its place on New Year's Day.

**A TANG BANQUET**
These elegant ladies of the Tang court are sitting down to a feast. They are accompanied by music and singing, but there are no men present – women and men usually ate separately. This painting dates from the AD900s, when raised tables came into fashion in China. Guests at banquets would wear their finest clothes. The most honoured guest would sit to the east of the host, who sat facing the south. The greatest honour of all was to be invited to dine with the emperor.

## MAKE RED BEAN SOUP

*You will need: measuring jug, scales, measuring spoon, 225g aduki beans, 3 tsp ground nuts, 4 tsp short-grain rice, cold water, tangerine, saucepan and lid, wooden spoon, 175g sugar, liquidizer, sieve, bowls.*

**1** Use the scales to weigh out the aduki beans. Add the ground nuts and the short-grain rice. Measure out 1 litre of cold water in the jug.

**2** Wash and drain the beans and rice. Put them in a bowl. Add the cold water. Leave overnight to soak. Do not drain off the water.

**3** Wash and dry the tangerine. Then carefully take off the peel in a continuous strip. Leave the peel overnight, until it is hard and dry.

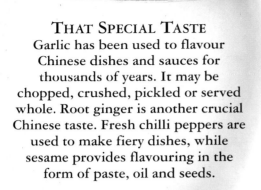

## THAT SPECIAL TASTE

Garlic has been used to flavour Chinese dishes and sauces for thousands of years. It may be chopped, crushed, pickled or served whole. Root ginger is another crucial Chinese taste. Fresh chilli peppers are used to make fiery dishes, while sesame provides flavouring in the form of paste, oil and seeds.

*sesame*

*root ginger*

## SHANG BRONZEWARE FIT FOR A FEAST

This three-legged bronze cooking pot dates from the Shang dynasty (*c.*1600BC–1122BC). Its green appearance is caused by the reaction of the metal to air over the 3,500 years since it was made. During Shang rule, metalworkers made many vessels out of bronze, including cooking pots and wine jars. They were used in all sorts of ceremonies, and at feasts people held in honour of their dead ancestors.

## BUTCHERS AT WORK

The stone carving (*shown right*) shows farmers butchering cattle in about AD50. In early China, cooks would cut up meat with square-shaped cleavers. It was then flavoured with wines and spices, and simmered in big pots over open fires until tender.

*Most peasant farmers lived on a simple diet. Red bean soup with rice was a typical daily meal. Herbs and spices were often added to make the food taste more interesting.*

**4** Put the soaked beans and rice (plus the soaking liquid) into a large saucepan. Add the dried tangerine peel and 500ml of cold water.

**5** Bring the mixture to the boil. Reduce the heat, cover the saucepan and simmer for 2 hours. Stir occasionally. If the liquid boils off, add more water.

**6** Weigh out the sugar. When the beans are just covered by water, add the sugar. Simmer until the sugar has completely dissolved.

**7** Remove and discard the tangerine peel. Leave soup to cool, uncovered. Liquidize the mixture. Strain any lumps with a sieve. Pour into bowls.

# Markets and Trade

THE EARLIEST CHINESE TRADERS used to barter (exchange) goods, but by 1600BC people were finding it easier to use tokens such as shells for buying and selling. The first metal coins date from about 750BC and were shaped like knives and spades. It was Qin Shi Huangdi, the first emperor, who introduced round coins. These had holes in the middle so that they could be threaded on to a cord for safe-keeping. The world's first paper money appeared in China in about AD900.

There were busy markets in every Chinese town, selling fruit, vegetables, rice, flour, eggs and poultry as well as cloth, medicine, pots and pans. In the Tang dynasty capital Chang'an (Xian), trading was limited to two large areas – the West Market and the East Market. This was so that government officials could control prices and trading standards.

### CHINESE TRADING
Goods from China changed hands many times on the Silk Road to Europe. Trade moved in both directions. Porcelain, tea and silk were carried westwards. Silver, gold and precious stones were transported back into China from central and southern Asia.

*raw silk*      *Chinese tea*

### CASH CROPS
Tea is trampled into chests in this European view of tea production in China. The work looks hard and the conditions cramped. For years China had traded with India and Arabia. In the 1500s it began a continuous trading relationship with Europe. By the early 1800s, China supplied 90 per cent of all the world's tea.

### MAKE A PELLET DRUM

*You will need: large roll of masking tape, pencil, thin cream card, thick card, scissors, glue and brush, 2.5cm x 30cm thin grey card, thread, ruler, needle, bamboo stick, paint (red, green and black), water pot, paintbrush, 2 coloured beads.*

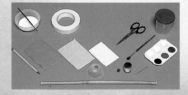

**1** Use the outside of the tape roll to draw 2 circles on thin cream card. Use the inside to draw 2 smaller circles on thick card. Cut out, as shown.

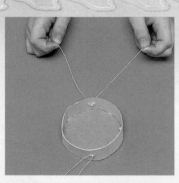

**2** Glue grey strip around one of smaller circles. Make 2 small holes each side of strip. Cut two 20cm threads. Pass through holes and knot.

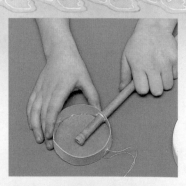

**3** Use the scissors to make a hole in the side of the strip for the bamboo stick. Push the stick through, as shown. Tape the stick to the hole.

## THE SILK ROAD

The trading route known as the Silk Road developed during the Han dynasty. The road ran for 11,000 kilometres from Chang'an (modern Xian), through Yumen and Kasghar, to Persia and the shores of the Mediterranean Sea. Merchants carried tea, silk and other goods from one trading post to the next.

## FROM DISTANT LANDS

A foreign trader rides on his camel during the Tang dynasty. At this time, China's international trade began to grow rapidly. Most trade was still handled by foreign merchants, among them Armenians, Jews and Persians. They traded their wares along the Silk Road, bringing goods to the court at the Tang dynasty capital, Chang'an.

## BUYERS AND SELLERS

This picture shows a typical Chinese market in about 1100. It appears on a Song dynasty scroll and is thought to show the market in the capital, Kaifeng, at the time of the New Year festival.

*Twist the drum handle to make the little balls rattle. In the hubbub of a street market, a merchant could shake a pellet drum to gain the attention of passers by. He would literally drum up trade!*

**4** Tape the stick handle down securely at the top of the drum. Take the second small circle and glue it firmly into place. This seals the drum.

**5** Draw matching designs of your choice on the 2 thin cream card circles. Cut out a decorative edge. Paint in the designs and leave them to dry.

**6** Paint the bamboo stick handle red and leave to dry. When the stick is dry, glue the 2 decorated circles into position on top of the 2 smaller circles.

**7** Thread on the 2 beads. Make sure the thread is long enough to allow the beads to hit the centre of the drum. Tie as shown. Cut off any excess.

# Medicine and Science

Fᴏᴍ ᴛʜᴇ ᴇᴍᴘɪʀᴇ'ꜱ earliest days, Chinese scholars published studies on medicine, astronomy and mathematics. The Chinese system of medicine had a similar aim to that of Daoist teachings, in that it attempted to make the body work harmoniously. The effects of all kinds of herbs, plants and animal parts were studied and then used to produce medicines. Acupuncture, which involves piercing the body with fine needles, was practised from about 2700BC. It was believed to release blocked channels of energy and so relieve pain.

The Chinese were also excellent mathematicians, and from 300BC they used a decimal system of counting based on tens. They may have invented the abacus, an early form of calculator, as well. In about 3000BC, Chinese astronomers produced a detailed chart of the heavens carved in stone. Later, they were the first to make observations of sunspots and exploding stars.

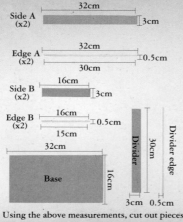

### NEW ILLS, OLD REMEDIES
A pharmacist weighs out a traditional medicine. Hundreds of medicines used in China today go back to ancient times. Many are herbal remedies later proved to work by scientists. Doctors are still researching their uses. Other traditional medicines are of less certain value, but are still popular purchases at street stalls.

### PRICKING POINTS
Acupuncturists used charts (*shown above*) to show exactly where to position their needles. The vital *qi* (energy) was thought to flow through the body along 12 lines called meridians. The health of the patient was judged by taking their pulse. Chinese acupuncture is practised all over the world today.

## MAKE AN ABACUS
*You will need: thick and thin card, ruler, pencil, scissors, wood glue and brush, masking tape, self-drying clay, cutting board, modelling tool, 30cm x 0.5cm dowel (x11), paintbrush, water pot, brown paint.*

Side A (x2) — 32cm — 3cm
Edge A (x2) — 32cm — 30cm — 0.5cm
Side B (x2) — 16cm — 3cm
Edge B (x2) — 16cm — 15cm — 0.5cm
Base — 32cm — 16cm
Divider — Divider edge — 30cm — 3cm — 0.5cm

Using the above measurements, cut out pieces from thick brown card and thin grey card. (pieces not shown to scale).

**1** Glue sides A and B to the base. Hold the edges with masking tape until dry. Then glue edges A and B to the tops of the sides, as shown.

**2** Roll the clay into a 2cm diameter sausage. Cut it into 77 small, flat beads. Make a hole through the centre of each bead with a dowel.

## A STREET DOCTOR PEDDLES HIS WARES

This European view of Chinese medicine dates from 1843.
It shows snakes and all sorts of unusual potions being sold on
the streets. The doctor is telling the crowd of miraculous cures.

## BURNING CURES

A country doctor
treats a patient with
traditional techniques
during the Song
dynasty. Chinese
doctors relieved pain
by heating parts of the
body with the burning
leaves of a plant called
moxa (mugwort).
The process is
called moxibustion.

## NATURAL HEALTH

Roots, seeds, leaves and flowers
have been used in Chinese medicine
for over 2,000 years. Today, nine out
of ten Chinese medicines are herbal
remedies. The Chinese yam is used
to treat exhaustion. Ginseng root is
used to help treat dizzy spells,
while mulberry wood is said to
lower blood pressure.

*Chinese yam*

*ginseng root*

*The abacus is an ancient
counting frame that acts as
a simple but very effective
calculator. Using an abacus,
Chinese mathematicians
and merchants could carry
out very difficult
calculations quickly
and easily.*

**3** Make 11 evenly spaced holes
in the divider. Edge one side
with thin card. Thread a dowel
through each hole. Paint all of
the abacus parts. Leave to dry.

**4** Thread 7 beads on to each
dowel rod – 2 on the upper
side of the divider, 5 on the
lower. Carefully fit the beads
and rods into the main frame.

**5** Each upper bead on the
abacus equals 5 lower beads
in the same column. Each lower
bead is worth 10 of the lower
beads in the column to its right.

**6** Here is a simple sum. To
calculate 5+3, first move
down one upper bead (worth 5).
Then move 3 lower beads in the
same column up (each worth 1).

# Feats of Engineering

THE ENGINEERING WONDER of ancient China was the Great Wall. It was known as *Wan Li Chang Cheng*, or the Wall of Ten Thousand *Li* (a unit of length). The Great Wall's total length was an incredible 6,400 kilometres. Work began on the wall in the 400s BC and lasted until the AD1500s. Its purpose was to protect China's borders from the fierce tribes who lived to the north. Despite this intention, Mongol invaders managed to breach its defences time after time. However, the Great Wall did serve as a useful communications route. It also extended the Chinese empire's control over a very long distance.

The Grand Canal is another engineering project that amazes us today. It was started in the 400s BC, but was mostly built during the Sui dynasty (AD581–618). Its aim was to link the north of China with the rice-growing regions in the south via the Chang Jiang (Yangzi River). It is still in use and runs northwards from Hangzhou to Beijing, a distance of 1,794 kilometres. Other great engineering feats were made by Chinese mining engineers, who were already digging deep mine shafts with drainage and ventilation systems in about 160BC.

**LIFE IN THE SALT MINES**
Workers busily excavate and purify salt from an underground mine. Inside a tower (*shown bottom left*) you can see workers using a pulley to raise baskets of mined salt. The picture comes from a relief (raised carving) found inside a Han dynasty tomb in the province of Sichuan.

**MINING ENGINEERING**
A Qing dynasty official tours an open-cast coalmine in the 1800s. China has rich natural resources and may have been the first country in the world to mine coal to burn as a fuel. Coal was probably discovered in about 200BC in what is now Jiangxi province. Other mines extracted metals and valuable minerals needed for the great empire. In the Han dynasty engineers invented methods of drilling boreholes to extract brine (salty water) from the ground. They also used derricks (rigid frame-works) to support iron drills – over 1,800 years before engineers in other parts of the world.

## HARD LABOUR

Peasants use their spades to dig roads instead of fields. Imperial China produced its great building and engineering works without the machines we rely on today. For big projects, workforces could number hundreds of thousands. Dangerous working conditions and a harsh climate killed many labourers.

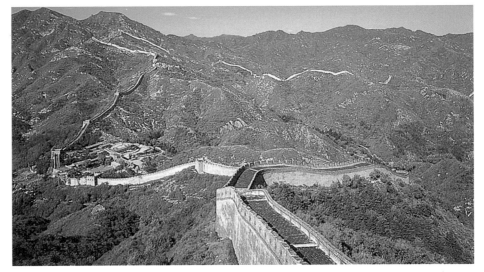

## BUILDING THE WALL

The Great Wall snakes over mountain ridges at Badaling, to the northwest of Beijing. The Great Wall and Grand Canal were built by millions of workers. All men aged between 23 and 56 were called up to work on them for one month each year. Only noblemen and civil servants were exempt.

## A GRAND OPENING

This painting from the 1700s imagines the Sui emperor Yangdi opening the first stage of the Grand Canal. Most of the work on this massive engineering project was carried out from AD605–609. A road was also built along the route. The transport network built up during the Sui dynasty (AD561–618) enabled food and other supplies to be moved easily from one part of the empire to another.

## THE CITY OF SIX THOUSAND BRIDGES

The reports about China supposedly made by Marco Polo in the 1200s described 6,000 bridges in the city of Suzhou. The Baodai Bridge (*shown above*) is one of them. It has 53 arches and was built between AD618 and AD906 to run across the Grand Canal.

# Famous Inventions

WHEN YOU WALK DOWN a shopping street in any modern city, it is very difficult to avoid seeing some object that was invented in China long ago. Printed words on paper, silk scarves, umbrellas or locks and keys are all Chinese innovations. Over the centuries, Chinese ingenuity and technical skill have changed the world in which we live.

A seismoscope is a very useful instrument in an earthquake-prone country such as China. It was invented in AD132 by a Chinese scientist called Zhang Heng. It could record the direction of even a distant earth tremor. Another key invention was the magnetic compass. In about AD1–100 the Chinese discovered that lodestone (a type of iron ore) could be made to point north. They realized that they could magnetize needles to do the same. By about AD1000, they worked out the difference between true north and magnetic north and began using compasses to keep ships on course.

Gunpowder is a Chinese invention from about AD850. At first it was used to blast rocks apart and to make fireworks. Later, it also began to be used in warfare.

**SHADE AND SHELTER**
A Qing dynasty woman uses an umbrella as a sunshade to protect her skin. The Chinese invented umbrellas about 1,600 years ago and they soon spread throughout the rest of Asia. Umbrellas became fashionable with both women and men and were regarded as a symbol of high rank.

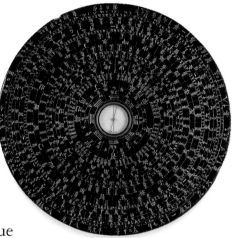

**THE SAILOR'S FRIEND**
The magnetic compass was invented in China in about AD1–100. At first it was used as a planning aid to ensure new houses faced in a direction that was in harmony with nature. Later it was used to plot courses on long sea voyages.

## MAKE A WHEELBARROW

*You will need: thick card, ruler, pencil, scissors, compasses, 0.5cm diameter balsa strips, glue and brush, paintbrush, paint (black and brown), water pot, 3.5cm x 0.5cm dowel, 2cm diameter rubber washers (x4).*

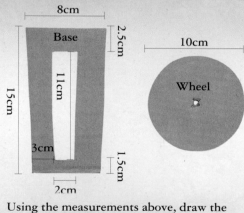

8cm

Base

2.5cm

15cm

11cm

3cm

2cm

1.5cm

10cm

Wheel

Using the measurements above, draw the pieces on to thick card. Draw the wheel with the compasses. Cut out pieces with scissors.

**1** Cut 7cm, 8cm and 26cm (x2) balsa strips. Glue 7cm strip to short edge of base and 8cm strip to top edge. Glue 26cm strips to side of base.

## SU SONG'S MASTERPIECE

This fantastic machine is a clock tower that can tell the time, chime the hours and follow the movement of the planets around the Sun. It was designed by an official called Su Song, in the city of Kaifeng in AD1092. The machine uses a mechanism called an escapement, which controls and regulates the timing of the clock. The escapement mechanism was invented in the AD700s by a Chinese inventor called Yi Xing.

## EARTHQUAKE WARNING

The decorative object shown above is the scientist Zhang Heng's seismoscope. When there was an earthquake, a ball was released from one of the dragons and fell into a frog's mouth. This showed the direction of the vibrations. According to records, in AD138 the instrument detected an earth tremor some 500 kilometres away.

## ONE-WHEELED TRANSPORT

In about AD100, the Chinese invented the wheelbarrow. They then designed a model with a large central wheel that could bear great weights. This became a form of transport, pushed along by muscle power.

*The single wheelbarrow was used by farmers and gardeners. Traders wheeled their goods to market, then used the barrow as a stall. They would sell a variety of goods, such as seeds, grain, plants and dried herbs.*

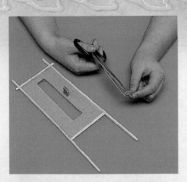

**2** Turn the base over. Cut two 2cm x 1cm pieces of thick card. Make a small hole in the middle of each, for the wheel axle. Glue pieces to base.

**3** Use compasses and a pencil to draw 1 circle around centre of wheel and 1 close to the rim. Mark on spokes. Paint spaces between spokes black.

**4** Paint the barrow, leave to dry. Cut two 7cm balsa strips with tapered ends to make legs, and paint them brown. When dry, glue to bottom of barrow.

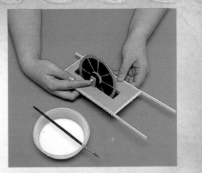

**5** Feed dowel axle between axle supports, via 2 washers, wheel, and 2 more washers. Dab glue on ends of axle to keep the wheel in place.

# Workers of Metal

THE CHINESE MASTERED THE secrets of making alloys (mixtures of two or more metals) during the Shang dynasty (c.1600BC–1122BC). They made bronze by melting copper and tin to separate each metal from its ore, a process called smelting. Nine parts of copper were then mixed with one part of tin and heated in a charcoal furnace. When the metals melted they were piped off into clay moulds. Bronze was used to make objects such as ceremonial pots, statues, bells, mirrors, tools and weapons.

By about 600BC the Chinese were smelting iron ore. They then became the first people to make cast iron by adding carbon to the molten metal. Cast iron is a tougher metal than bronze and it was soon being used to make weapons, tools and plough blades. By AD1000 the Chinese were mining and working a vast amount of iron. Coke (a type of coal) had replaced the charcoal used in furnaces, which were fired up by water-driven bellows. Chinese metal workers also produced delicate gold and silver ornaments set with precious stones.

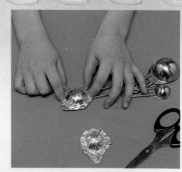

**SILVER SCISSORS**
This pair of scissors is made of silver. They are proof of the foreign influences that entered China in the AD700s, during the boom years of the Tang dynasty. The metal is beaten, rather than cast in the Chinese way. It is decorated in the Persian style of the Silk Road, with engraving and punching.

**BEWARE OF THE LION**
This gilded *fo* (Buddhist) lion guards the halls and chambers of Beijing's imperial palace, the Forbidden City. It is one of a fearsome collection of bronze guardian figures, including statues of dragons and turtles.

## MAKE A NECKLACE

*You will need: tape measure, thick wire, thin wire, masking tape, scissors, tin foil, measuring spoon, glue and brush, fuse wire.*

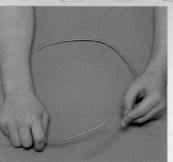

1 Measure around your neck using a tape measure. Ask an adult to cut a piece of thick wire to 1½ times this length. Shape it into a rough circle.

2 Cut two 4cm pieces of thin wire. Coil loosely around sides of thick wire. Tape ends to thick wire. Slide thick wire through coils to adjust fit.

3 Cut out an oval-shaped piece of tin foil. Shape it into a pendant half, using a measuring spoon or teaspoon. Make 9 more halves.

## MINERAL WEALTH

The Chinese probably learnt to smelt ore in furnaces from their experience with high-temperature pottery kilns. The land was rich in copper, tin and iron, and the Chinese were very skilled miners. Large amounts of precious metals, such as gold and silver, had to be imported.

*gold nugget*    *silver ore*

## PEACE BE WITH YOU

The Hall of Supreme Harmony in Beijing's Forbidden City is guarded by this bronze statue of a turtle. Despite its rather fearsome appearance, the turtle was actually a symbol of peace.

## DECORATIVE PROTECTION

These nail protectors are made of gold, with inlaid feathers. They were worn by the Empress Dowager Cixi in the 1800s to stop her 15-cm-long little fingernails breaking.

## GOLDEN FIREBIRDS

Chinese craftsmen fashioned these beautiful phoenix birds from thin sheets of delicate gold. The mythical Arabian phoenix was said to set fire to its nest and die, only to rise again from the ashes. During the Tang dynasty the phoenix became a symbol of the Chinese empress Wu Zetian, who came to power in AD660. It later came to be a more general symbol for all empresses.

4 Glue the 2 pendant halves together, leaving one end open. Drop some rolled-up balls of foil into the opening. Seal the opening with glue.

5 Make 4 more pendants in the same way. Thread each pendant on to the neckband with pieces of thin fuse wire. Leave a gap between each one.

*People of all classes wore decorative jewellery in imperial China. The design of this necklace is based on the metal bell bracelets worn by Chinese children.*

# Porcelain and Lacquer

ALTHOUGH POTTERY FIRST developed in Japan and parts of western Asia, Chinese potters were hard at work over 6,000 years ago. In 3200BC, clay was being fired (baked) in kilns at about 900°C.

By 1400BC, potters were making beautiful, white stoneware, baked at much higher temperatures. Shiny glazes were developed to coat the fired clay. Later, the Chinese invented porcelain, the finest, most delicate pottery of all. It was to become one of China's most important exports to other parts of Asia and Europe. In the English language, the word china is used for all fine-quality pottery.

The Chinese were the first to use lacquer. This plastic-like material is a natural substance from the sap of a tree that grows in China. The sap makes a smooth, hard varnish. From about 1300BC onwards, lacquer was used for coating wooden surfaces, such as house timbers, bowls or furniture. It could also be applied to leather and metal. Natural lacquer is grey, but in China pigment was added to make it black or bright red. It was applied in many layers until thick enough to be carved or inlaid with mother-of-pearl.

### ENAMEL WARE
Ming dynasty craft workers made this ornate flask. It is covered with a glassy material called enamel, set inside thin metal wire. This technique, called cloisonné (partitioned), was introduced from Persia.

### CHINA'S HISTORY TOLD ON THE BIG SCREEN
This beautifully detailed, glossy lacquer screen shows a group of Portuguese merchants on a visit to China. It was made in the 1600s. Chinese crafts first became popular in Europe at this time, as European traders began doing business in southern China's ports.

### FLORAL BOTTLE
This attractive Ming dynasty bottle is decorated with a coating of bright red lacquer. The lacquer is coloured with a mineral called cinnabar. It would have taken many long hours to apply and dry the many layers of lacquer. The bottle is carved with a design of peonies, which were a very popular flower in China.

## FISH ON A PLATE

Pictures of fish decorate the border of this precious porcelain plate. It was made during the reign of the Qing emperor Yongzheng (1722–1736), a period famous for its elegant designs. It is coloured with enamel. Porcelain is made from a fine white clay called kaolin (china clay) and a mineral called feldspar. They are fired (baked) to a very high temperature.

## A JUG OF WINE

An unknown Chinese potter made this beautiful wine jug about 1,000 years ago. It has been fired to such a high temperature that it has become glassy stoneware. It is coated with a grey-green glaze called celadon.

## LIFE-LIKE FIGURES

A Ming dynasty entertainer smiles at his audience. All sorts of pottery figures have been found in Ming dynasty tombs. Potters made lively figures of merchants, musicians, court ladies and animals. Some are comic, while others are beautiful.

## DEEP BLUE, PURE WHITE

These blue-and-white vases are typical of the late Ming dynasty (1368–1644). In the 1600s large numbers were exported to Europe. Many were produced at the imperial potteries at Jingdezhen, in northern Jiangxi province. These workshops were set up in 1369, as the region had plentiful supplies of the very best clay. Some of the finest pottery ever made was produced there in the 1400s and 1500s.

# The Secret of Silk

FOR YEARS, THE CHINESE tried to stop outsiders finding out how they made their most popular export – *si*, or silk. The shimmering colours and smooth textures of Chinese silk made it the wonder of the ancient world. Other countries such as India discovered the secret of silk making, but China remained the producer of the world's best silk.

Silk production probably dates back to late Stone Age times (8000BC–2500BC) in China. Legend says that the process was invented by the empress Lei Zu in about 2640BC. Silkworms (the caterpillars of a type of moth) are kept on trays and fed on the leaves of white mulberry trees. The silkworms spin a cocoon (casing) of fine but very strong filaments. The cocoons are plunged into boiling water to separate the filaments, which are then carefully wound on to reels.

A filament of silk can be up to 1,200 metres long. Several filaments are spun together to make up thread, which is then woven into cloth on a loom. The Chinese used silk to make all kinds of beautiful products. They learned to weave flimsy gauzes and rich brocades, and they then wove elaborate coloured patterns into the cloth in a style known as *ke si*, or cut silk.

### PREPARING THE THREAD
A young woman winds silk thread on to bobbins in the late 1700s. Up to 30 filaments of silk could be twisted together to make silk thread for weaving. The Chinese made ingenious equipment for spinning silk into thread. They also built looms for weaving thread into large rolls of fabric. By the 1600s, the city of Nanjing alone had an estimated 50,000 looms.

### LOAD THOSE BALES!
Workers at a Chinese silk factory of the 1840s carry large bales of woven silk down to the jetty. From there the woven cloth would be shipped to the city. It might be used to make a costume for a lady of the court, or else exported abroad. The Chinese silk industry reached its peak of prosperity in the mid-1800s.

## WINDING SILK
Silk is being prepared at this workshop of the 1600s. The workers are taking filaments (threads) from the cocoons and winding them on to a reel. Traditionally, the chief areas of silk production in imperial China were in the east coast provinces of Zhejiang and Jiangsu. Silk was also produced in large quantities in Sichuan, in the west.

## THE DRAGON ON THE EMPEROR'S BACK
A scaly red dragon writhes across a sea of yellow silk. The dragon was embroidered on to a robe for an emperor of the Qing dynasty. The exquisite clothes made for the Chinese imperial court at this time are considered to be great works of art.

## MAKING SILK
Raising silkworms is called sericulture. It can be a complicated business. The caterpillars have to be kept at a controlled temperature for a month before they begin spinning their silk cocoons.

*adult silkmoth and cocoons*

*silkmoth larva*

## MAGIC MULBERRIES
These Han dynasty workers are collecting mulberry leaves in big baskets, over 2,000 years ago. These would have been used to feed the silkworms. Silkworms are actually the larva (caterpillars) of a kind of moth. Like most caterpillars, silkworms are fussy feeders and will only eat certain kinds of plant before they spin cocoons.

# Dress and Ornament

CHINESE PEASANTS dressed in simple clothes made from basic materials. They mostly wore cotton tunics over loose trousers, with sandals made of rushes or straw. In the south, broad-brimmed, cone-shaped hats helped to protect the wearer from the hot sun and heavy rain. In the north, fur hats, sheepskins and quilted jackets were worn to keep out the cold. Rich people often dressed in elaborate, expensive clothes. Government officials wore special robes that reflected their rank and status. Beautiful silk robes patterned with dragons (*lung pao*) were worn by court ladies, officials, and the emperor himself.

Court dress varied greatly over the ages. Foreign invasions brought new fashions and dress codes. Under the Manchus, who ruled as the Qing dynasty from AD1644, men had to wear a long pigtail. Rich people grew their little fingernails so long that special nail guards were worn to prevent them from breaking off.

**MONKEY PENDANT**
Wealthy people often wore very expensive, well-crafted jewellery. This beautiful piece from the AD700s is a pendant necklace. It could have been worn by both men and women. The pendant is made from white jade set in a beaded frame of gilded bronze.

**CLOTHES FIT FOR AN EMPEROR**
This magnificent imperial robe was made from interwoven, heavy silks in the 1800s. The narrow sleeves, with their horse hoof cuffs, are typical of the Qing dynasty.

**FASTEN YOUR BELT**
Belt hooks and buckles became an essential part of noblemen's clothing from about the 300s BC. They were highly decorated, and made of bronze.

## MAKE A FAN

*You will need: masking tape, red tissue paper, thick card base, ruler, pencil, compasses, paint (pink, light blue, cream, light green), thin paintbrush, water pot, scissors, 16cm x 1cm balsa strips (x15), barbecue stick, glue and brush, thin card.*

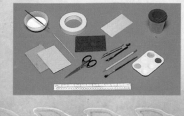

**1** Tape tissue paper on to base. Make a compass hole 1cm from the edge. From this mark, draw a 16cm radius semicircle and a 7cm radius semicircle.

**2** Place one end of the ruler at compass hole. Mark the point with a pencil. Draw evenly spaced lines 1cm apart between the semi-circles.

**3** Draw your design on to the tissue paper. Paint in the details. Allow to dry. Remove paper from base. Cut out fan along edges of the semicircles.

## OFFICIAL DRESS

A well-dressed civil servant cools down in the summer heat. Chinese government officials wore elegant clothes that showed their social rank. This picture was painted by a European artist in about 1800. The official is wearing his summer outfit, which consists of a long narrow-sleeved tunic, slippers and a brimmed hat. It is a hot day, so he also carries a fan to provide a cool breeze.

## LADIES OF THE COURT

These Tang ladies are dressed in the high fashion of the AD700s. Silk was the material worn by the nobles of the day, and court costume included long robes and skirts, various tunics and sashes. The clothes were often beautifully decorated, with colourful patterns and elaborate designs.

## ADDED STYLE

Over the ages, all kinds of accessories became part of Chinese costume. These included elaborate hats and headdresses for men and women, sunshades, fans, belts and buckles. Tiny leather shoes lined with silk were worn by noble women.

*ladies' shoes*

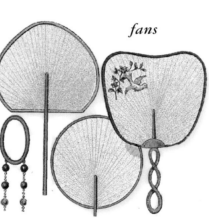

*fans*

*earring*

*The earliest Chinese fans were made of feathers or of silk stretched over a flat frame. In about AD1000 folding fans were introduced into China, probably from Japan.*

**4** Using scissors, cut each balsa strip 1cm narrower (0.5cm each side) for half of its length. Make a compass hole at the base of each strip.

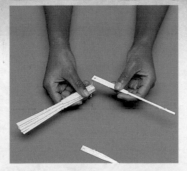

**5** Stack strips. Pass a barbecue stick through holes. It must be long enough to fit through and overlap either side. Make sure strips can move freely.

**6** Fold the paper backwards and forwards to form a concertina. Glue each alternate fold of the paper to the narrow ends of the strips, as shown.

**7** Paint the top strip of the fan pink. Allow to dry. Cut out small card discs. Glue them over the ends of the barbecue stick to secure the strips.

# Chinese Art

In imperial China, painting was believed to be the finest of all the arts. It was considered to be a mark of civilization and a suitable pastime for scholars and even emperors. Painting was based upon the same ideas of harmony and simplicity that were important in the Daoist and Buddhist faiths. Paintings appeared on scrolls of silk and paper, walls, screens and fans. Popular subjects for pictures varied over the ages. They included the misty mountains and rivers of southern China, as well as landscapes set off by lone human figures. Artists also painted birds, animals and plants, such as bamboo or lotus. Sometimes just a few brush strokes were used to capture the spirit of the subject. Chinese writing in the form of a poem often played an important part in many pictures. Chinese artists also produced woodcuts, which are prints made from a carved wooden block. Traditionally these were not valued as much as the paintings, but many beautiful woodcuts were produced during the reign of the Ming dynasty (1368–1644).

**SYMBOLS OF WISDOM**
To the Chinese, the dragon embodied wisdom, strength and goodness. This intricate ivory seal belonged to a Ming emperor and shows a dragon guarding the pearl of wisdom.

**WINDOW ON THE PAST**
A royal procession makes its way along a mountain range. This detail from a painting on silk is by the great master Li Sixun (AD651–716). Many Tang dynasty paintings show court life and royal processions, but they are far from dull. They provide a colourful glimpse of life in China at that time. This picture shows what people wore and how they travelled.

## MAKE PAPER CUT-OUTS
*You will need: A4 sized coloured paper, pencil, ruler, scissors.*

1 Take a piece of coloured paper and lay it flat on a hard surface. Fold it exactly in half widthways. Make a firm crease along the fold, as shown above.

2 Draw a Chinese-style design on the paper. Make sure all the shapes meet up at the fold. Make a tracing of your design so you can use it again.

3 Keeping card folded, cut out shapes. Make sure you don't cut along the folded edge. Cut away areas you want to discard in between the shapes.

## AT FULL GALLOP

Chinese artists greatly admired horses and loved to try to capture their strength and movement in paintings. This lively wall painting was found in a Han dynasty tomb.

## PAINTING NATURE

Morning mist hangs over a mountain backdrop. This detail from a masterpiece by Qiu Ying (1494–1552) is inspired by the forests and mountain landscapes of his homeland. Artists such as Qiu Ying were successful and well paid.

## ART IN PORCELAIN

China's craft workers and designers were also great artists. This blue-and-white porcelain wine jar was made in the 1600s in the form of a mandarin duck and drake. Its hand-painted details would have taken many long hours of work to complete. Blue-and-white porcelain was very popular during the Ming dynasty.

## SPRINGTIME ON PAPER

A watercolour painting from the 1800s shows peach blossom just as it comes into flower. It is painted in a very realistic, fresh and simple style. This approach is a common characteristic of much Chinese art.

4 Now open up your design. Be careful not to tear it. To add details to the figures, fold paper again. Mark the details to be cut along the crease.

5 Using a pair of scissors, carefully cut out the detail along the crease. The cut-out detail will be matched perfectly on the other side of the figure.

*Carefully open up your finished cut-out. Display the design by sticking it to a window, so that light shines through. In China, paper cut-outs are traditionally used to bring luck and good fortune.*

# The Written Word

THE CHINESE LANGUAGE is written with symbols called characters, which stand for sounds and words. They have changed and developed over the ages. A dictionary published in 1716 lists over 40,000 of them. Each character was written by hand with a brush, using 11 basic brush strokes. The painting of these beautiful characters is called calligraphy, and was always seen as a form of art.

The Chinese began using woodblocks for printing in about 1600BC. Before that, books had often been handwritten on bamboo strips. Ancient Chinese writers produced all sorts of practical handbooks and encyclopedias. Poetry first developed about 3,000 years ago. It was the Chinese who invented paper, nearly 2,000 years ago. Cloth or bark was shredded, pulped and dried on frames. Movable type was invented in the 1040s. During the 1500s popular folk tales such as *The Water Margin* were published, and in the 1700s the writer Cao Xuequin produced China's greatest novel, *A Dream of Red Mansions.*

**MAGICAL MESSAGES**
The earliest surviving Chinese script appears on animal bones. They were used for telling fortunes in about 1200BC. The script was made up of small pictures representing objects or ideas. Modern Chinese script is made up of patterns of lines.

**ART OF CALLIGRAPHY**
This text was handwritten during the Tang dynasty (AD618–906). Traditional Chinese writing reads down from right to left, starting in the top right-hand corner.

漢興六十餘載海
內乂安府庫充實
而四歲未賔制度
多求闕上方欲用文
而肉荄主父公蒲
之式技於買於寵
擇於奴僕亦弟
漢之得人於茲為盛
董仲舒石建石慶
則韓安國鄭當時
定令則韓安國趙禹張湯
文章則司馬遷相如
如滑稽則東方朔枚皋
朱買臣則嚴助吾唐蒙

## MAKE PRINTING BLOCKS

*You will need: plain white paper, pencil, paint, soft Chinese brush or thin paintbrush, water pot, tracing paper, board, self-drying clay (15cm x 20cm, 2.5cm thick), modelling tool, wood glue, block printing ink, damp rag.*

**1** Copy or trace the characters from the reversed image block (see opposite). Start off with a pencil outline, then fill in with paint. Leave to dry.

**2** Copy design on to tracing paper. Turn the paper over. Place it on the clay. Scribble on the clean side of the paper to leave a mirror image in the clay.

**3** Use a modelling tool to carve out characters. Cut away clay all around characters to make a relief (raised pattern). Smooth clay base with your fingertips.

## THE BEST WAY TO WRITE

A calligrapher of the 1840s begins to write, surrounded by his assistants. The brush must be held upright for the writing of Chinese characters. The wrist is never rested on the table. Many years of practice and study are necessary to become a good calligrapher.

## THE PRINTED PAGE

The Buddhist scripture called the Diamond Sutra *(shown right)* is probably the oldest surviving printed book in the world. It includes both text and pictures. The book was printed from a woodblock on 11 May AD868 and was intended to be distributed at no cost to the public.

## INKS AND COLOURS

Watercolours and inks were based on plant and mineral pigments in reds, browns, blues, greens and yellows. Black ink was made from carbon, obtained from soot. This was mixed with glue to form a solid block. The ink block would be wetted during use. Brushes were made from animal hair fitted into bamboo handles.

*Chinese brushes*

*reversed image*   *actual image*

*Block rubbings of characters were an early form of printing.*

Moon  Ruler

Mouth  Sun

**4** When the relief has dried, paint the clay block with wood glue. Leave it to dry thoroughly. When dry, the glue seals and protects the pattern.

**5** Now paint the design. Apply a thick layer of printing ink to the raised parts of the clay with a Chinese brush or a soft paintbrush.

**6** Lay a thin piece of plain white paper over the inked block. Use a dry brush to press the paper into the ink, so that the paper takes up the design.

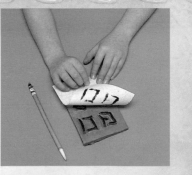

**7** Lift up the paper to reveal your design. Look after your printing block by cleaning it with a damp rag. You can then use it again and again.

# Musicians and Performers

THE EARLIEST CHINESE POETRY was sung rather than spoken. *Shijing* (the Book of Songs) dates back over 3,000 years and includes the words to hymns and folk songs. For most of China's history, musicians were employed in rich households. Orchestras played drums, gongs, pan pipes, racks of bronze bells, fiddles and other stringed instruments. Music was considered an important part of life, and models of musicians were often put in tombs to provide entertainment in the afterlife.

Musicians were frequently accompanied by acrobats, jugglers and magicians. Such acts were as popular in the markets and streets of the town as in the courtyards of nobles. Storytelling and puppet shows were equally well loved. Plays and opera became hugely popular in the AD1200s, with tales of murder, intrigue, heroism and love acted out to music. Most of the female roles would be played by men.

**THE COURT DANCER**
Arching her right arm upwards, an elegant dancer performs at the royal court. The model's flowing dress belongs to the fashions of the Tang dynasty (AD618–906).

**PUTTING ON A PUPPET SHOW**
Children put on a show with marionettes (puppets moved by strings) in the 1600s. Drumming was used to provide musical accompaniment, just like in a professional play of the period.

**MAKE A MASK**
*You will need: tape measure, large block of self-drying clay, board, modelling tool, petroleum jelly, newspaper, wood glue and brush, scissors, thick card, masking tape, 2 large white beads, paintbrush, paints (grey, cream, terracotta and yellow), water pot, needle, black wool, string.*

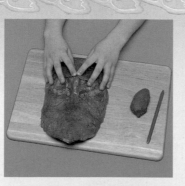

1 Measure the width and length of your face with a tape measure. Make a clay mould. Carve out the eyes and attach a clay nose to the mask.

2 Paint front of mask with petroleum jelly. Apply 4–6 layers of papier-mâché. This is made by soaking torn newspaper in water and glue. Leave to dry.

3 Remove mask from the clay mould. Cut a 2.5cm wide strip of card long enough to fit around your face. Bend it into a circle, and tape to the mask.

## MUSIC IN THE GARDEN

Musicians in the 1800s play *qins* (lutes) and *sheng* (flutes) in a garden setting. The music tried to reflect nature's harmony. It was intended to make the listener feel peaceful and spiritual.

## CHINESE OPERA

These stars of the Chinese opera are performing in the 1700s. Well-known folk tales were acted out to the dramatic sound of crashing cymbals and high-pitched singing. Elaborate make-up and fancy costumes made it clear to the audience whether the actor was playing a hero or a villain, a princess or a demon.

*Elaborate masks like these were worn to great effect in Chinese opera. When your mask is finished, you can wear it to scare your friends!*

## SOUND THE DRUMS!

The cavalcade that followed an important government official or general might have included mounted drummers or trumpeters. These figures of musicians on horseback were found in the tomb of a high-ranking official from the Tang dynasty.

**4** Cut 2 pointed ear shapes from card. Fold card at the edge to make flaps. Cut out and glue on small, decorative pieces of card. Glue ears to the mask.

**5** Glue on 2 large white beads for the eyes. Cut out more small pieces of card. Glue these on above the eyes. Add another piece of card for the lips.

**6** Paint the mask with the grey base colour first. Leave to dry. Then add details using the brighter colours. When dry, varnish with wood glue.

**7** Use a needle to thread black wool through for the beard. Tape wool to back of the mask. Thread string through side of mask behind ears to tie it on.

# Games and Pastimes

Fʀᴏᴍ ᴇᴀʀʟʏ ɪɴ Cʜɪɴᴀ's history, kings and nobles loved to go hunting for pleasure. Horses and chariots were used to hunt deer and wild boar. Dogs and even cheetahs were trained to chase the prey. Spears, bows and arrows were then used to kill it. Falconry (using birds of prey to hunt animals) was commonplace by about 2000BC.

In the Ming and Qing dynasties ancient spiritual disciplines used by Daoist monks were brought together with the battle training used by warriors. These martial arts (*wu shu*) were intended to train both mind and body. They came to include the body movements known as tai chi (*taijiquan*), sword play (*jianwu*) and the extreme combat known as kung fu (*gongfu*).

Archery was a popular sport in imperial China. The Chinese also loved gambling, and may have invented the first card games over 2,000 years ago.

### CHINESE CHESS
The traditional Chinese game of xiang qi is similar to western chess. One army battles against another, with round discs used as playing pieces. To tell the discs apart, each is marked with a name.

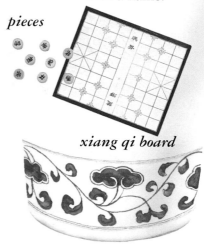

*pieces*

*xiang qi board*

### PEACE THROUGH MOVEMENT
A student of tai chi practises his art. The Chinese first developed the system of exercises known as tai chi more than 2,000 years ago. The techniques of tai chi were designed to help relax the human body and concentrate the mind.

---

### MAKE A KITE

*You will need: 30cm barbecue sticks (x12), ruler, scissors, glue and brush, plastic insulating tape, A1-size paper, pencil, paint (blue, red, yellow, black and pink), paintbrush, water pot, string, piece of wooden dowel, small metal ring.*

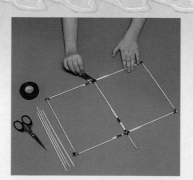

**1** Make a 40cm x 30cm rectangle by joining some of the sticks. Overlap the sticks for strength, then glue and tape together. Add a centre rod.

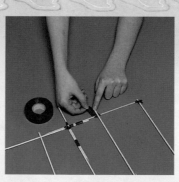

**2** Make another rectangle 15cm x 40cm long. Overlay the second rectangle on top of the first one. Tape rectangles together, as shown above.

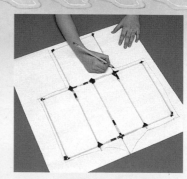

**3** Place frame on to a sheet of white A1-size paper. Draw a 2.5cm border around outside of frame. Add curves around the end of the centre rod.

## BAMBOO BETTING

Gamblers place bets in a game of *liu po.* Bamboo sticks were thrown like dice to decide how far the counters on the board should move. Gambling was a widespread pastime during the Han dynasty. People would bet large sums of money on the outcome of card games, horse races and cock fights.

## ALL-IN WRESTLING

This bronze figure of two wrestling muscle men was made in about 300BC. Wrestling was a very popular entertainment and sport in imperial China. It continues to be an attraction at country fairs and festivals.

## POLO PONIES

These women from the Tang dynasty are playing a fast and furious game of polo. They are probably noblewomen from the Emperor's royal court. The sport of polo was originally played in India and central Asia. It was invented as a training game to improve the riding skills of soldiers in cavalry units.

*Chinese children today still play with home-made paper kites. Kites were invented in China in about 400BC.*

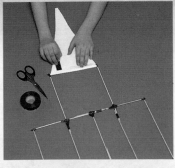

**4** Cut out the kite shape from the paper. Using a pencil, draw the details of your dragon design on the paper. Paint in your design and leave to dry.

**5** Cut a triangular piece of paper to hang from the end of your kite as a tail. Fold tail over rod at bottom of kite, as shown. Tape tail into position.

**6** Carefully tape and glue your design on to the frame. Fold over border that you allowed for when cutting out the paper. Tape to back of paper, as shown.

**7** Wrap 10m of string around dowel. Tie other end to ring. Pass 2 pieces of string through kite from the back. Tie to centre rod. Tie other ends to ring.

# Travel by Land

THE CHINESE EMPIRE was linked by a network of roads used only by the army, officials and royal messengers. A special carriageway was reserved for the emperor himself. Ordinary people travelled along dusty or muddy routes and tracks.

China's mountainous landscape and large number of rivers meant that Chinese engineers became expert at bridge-building. Suspension bridges made of rope and bamboo were being used from about AD1 onwards. A bridge suspended from iron chains crossed the Chang Jiang (Yangzi River) as early as AD580. A stone arch bridge built in about AD615 still stands today at Zhouxian in Hebei province. Most people travelled by foot and porters often had to carry great loads on their backs. They also carried wealthy people from place to place on litters (chairs).

China's small native ponies were interbred with larger, stronger horses from central Asia sometime after 100BC. This provided fast, powerful mounts that were suitable for messengers and officials, and they were also capable of pulling chariots and carriages. Mules and camels were widely used along the trade routes of the north, while shaggy yaks carried loads in the high mountains of the Himalayas. Carts were usually hauled along by oxen.

### HEADING OUT WEST
Chinese horsemen escort the camels of a caravan (trading expedition). The traders are about to set out along the Silk Road. This trading route ran all the way from Chang'an (Xian) in China right through to Europe and the lands of the Mediterranean.

### RIDING ON HORSEBACK
A Chinese nobleman from about 2,000 years ago reins in his elegant horse. Breaking in the horse would have been difficult, as the rider has no stirrups and could easily be unseated. Metal stirrups were in general use in China by AD302. They provided more stability and helped to improve the rider's control of the horse.

## CARRIED BY HAND
A lazy landowner of the Qing dynasty travels around his estates. He is carried along in a litter, a platform supported by the shoulders of his tired, long-suffering servants. An umbrella shades the landowner from the heat of the summer sun.

## CAMEL POWER
Bactrian (two-humped) camels were originally bred in central Asia. They could endure the extremes of heat and cold of the region, and travel for long distances without water. This toughness made them ideal for transporting goods along the Silk Road.

## HAN CARRIAGE
During the Han period, three-horse carriages were used by the imperial family only. This carving from a tomb brick is probably of a messenger carrying an important order from the emperor.

## TRAVELLING IN STYLE
During the Han dynasty, government officials travelled in stylish horse-drawn carriages. This picture is taken from a decorative brick found in a Han tomb. After larger, stronger breeds of horses were introduced into China from central Asia, the horse became a status symbol for the rich and powerful. Such horses were considered to be celestial (heavenly).

# Junks and Sampans

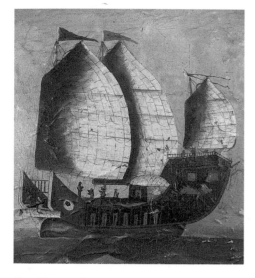

**IN FULL SAIL**
Junks were a type of sailing vessel used by merchants in the East and South China seas. They were also used by pirates. The China seas could be blue and peaceful, but they were often whipped into a fury by typhoons (tropical storms).

FROM EARLY IN CHINA'S history, its rivers, lakes and man-made canals were the country's main highways. Fishermen propelled small wooden boats across the water with a single oar or pole at the stern. These small boats were often roofed with mats, like the sampans (which means "three planks" in Chinese) still seen today. Large wooden sailing ships, which we call junks, sailed the open ocean. They were either keeled or flat-bottomed, with a high stern and square bows. Their sails were made of matting stiffened with strips of bamboo. By the AD800s, Chinese shipbuilders had built the first ships with several masts and proper rudders.

In the 1400s, admirals Zheng He and Wang Jinghong led seven sea expeditions that visited Southeast Asia, India, Arabia and East Africa. The flagship of their 300-strong naval fleet was over five times the size of the largest European ships of the time.

**RIVER TRAFFIC**
All sorts of small trading boats were sailed or rowed along China's rivers in the 1850s. River travel was often difficult and could be dangerous. Floods were common along the Huang He (Yellow River), which often changed course. The upper parts of China's longest river, the Chang Jiang (Yangzi River), were rocky and had powerful currents.

## MAKE A SAMPAN

*You will need: ruler, pencil, thick and thin card, scissors, glue and brush, masking tape, 6 wooden barbecue sticks, string, thin yellow paper, paint (black, dark brown), paintbrush, water pot.*

39cm — 1cm — Runner A (x2)
33.5cm — Side B (x2) — 5cm — 15cm
Base C (x2) — 15cm — 7cm — Base D — 18cm
Floor E — 7cm — 10cm — 4cm — Floor F (x2) — 7cm — Edge G (x2) — 1cm — 6.5cm

Cut pieces B, C, D and G from thick card. Cut pieces A, E, and F from thin card.

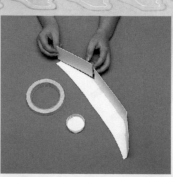

1 Glue base pieces C and D to side B, as shown. Hold the pieces with masking tape while the glue dries. When dry, remove the masking tape.

2 Glue remaining side B to the boat. Stick runner A pieces to top of the sides. Make sure the ends jut out 2.5cm at the front and back of the boat.

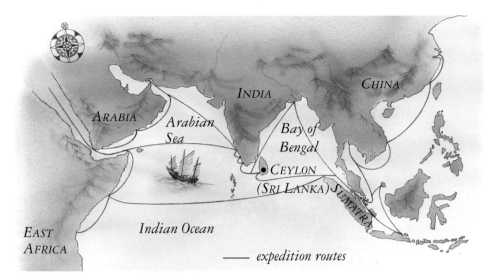

## FISHERMEN'S FEASTS

Seas, lakes and rivers were an important food source in imperial China. Drying fish was often the only way to preserve it in the days before refrigeration. Dried fish made strong-tasting sauces and soups. Popular seafoods included crabs, prawns and squid.

*dried fish*

*dried squid*

## THE VOYAGES OF ZHENG HE

Chinese admirals Zheng He and Wang Jinghong carried out seven fantastic voyages of exploration between 1405 and 1433. This map shows how far and wide they travelled on these expeditions. Their impressive fleets included over 60 ships crewed by about 27,000 seamen, officers and interpreters. The biggest of their vessels was 147 metres long and 60 metres wide.

## THE FISHING TRIP

A fisherman poles his boat across the river in the 1500s. The bird shown in the picture is a tamed cormorant, used for catching the fish. The cormorant was normally attached to a line, with a ring around its neck to prevent it from swallowing the fish.

*To add the finishing touch to your sampan, make a boatman and oar to propel the vessel through the waterways.*

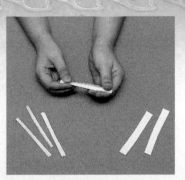

**3** Glue floor E to centre of base. Add floor F pieces to the ends of the base, as shown. Stick edge G pieces in between the ends of the runners.

**4** Bend 2 barbecue sticks into 10cm high arches. Cut 2 more sticks into five 10cm struts. Glue and tie 2 struts to sides of arches and 1 to the top.

**5** Repeat step 4 to make a second roof. To make roof matting, cut thin yellow paper into 1cm x 10cm strips. Fold strips in half and stick to roofs.

**6** Paint boat and roofs. Allow to dry. Glue the matting strips to the roofs, as shown. When the glue is dry, place roofs inside the boat.

# Soldiers and Weapons

IN CHINA'S EARLY HISTORY, bitter warfare between local rulers devastated the countryside with an appalling cost in human lives. Battle tactics and campaigns were discussed in *The Art of War* by Master Sun, who lived in the 500s BC at around the same time as the thinker Kong Fuzi (Confucius). This was the first book of its kind and its ideas are still studied today. After the empire was united in 221BC, rulers still needed large armies to stay in power and to guard against invasion.

The first Chinese armies fought with horse-drawn chariots and bronze weapons. Later, battles were fought with iron weapons, horsemen and hundreds of thousands of footsoldiers. Armour was made of metal, lacquered leather or padded quilting. Weapons included bows and arrows, powerful crossbows, swords and halberds (long blades on poles). As the empire grew, the Han Chinese came into conflict with the many peoples whose lands now lay in China.

### PRECIOUS SPEAR
This spearhead is over 3,200 years old. It was made from the precious stone jade set in bronze and turquoise. The spear was intended for ceremonial use, as it was far too precious to be used in combat.

### SOLDIER ON HORSEBACK
A Tang dynasty warrior sits astride his horse, ready for battle. His horse is also ready to fight, covered by a protective jacket. The warrior's feet are supported by stirrups. These were useful in combat, as they allowed a soldier to remain steady in the saddle as he fought.

## MAKE CHINESE ARMOUR

*You will need: 150cm x 70cm felt fabric, scissors, large sewing needle, string, silver card, ruler, pencil, tape, split pins, silver paint, paintbrush, water pot, thick card, glue and brush.*

1 Fold felt fabric in half. Cut a semicircle along fold to make a neck hole. Put garment on. Trim so it just reaches your hips and covers your shoulders.

2 Use scissors to make 2 holes either side of the waist. Pass string through holes. Secure as shown. The string will be used to tie the garment to your waist.

3 Cut 70 squares (5cm x 5cm) out of silver card. Lay a row of overlapping squares face down at the top of the fabric. Tape the rows together.

## FIGHTING ON THE GREAT WALL
In 1884–1885, heavily armed French soldiers engaged in battle with the Chinese. The empire was in decline by the 1880s, and its outdated tactics were no match for the superior might of the French forces.

## BATTLING HAN
This battered-looking helmet would once have protected a Han soldier's head from crossbow bolts, sword blows and arrows. Young men were conscripted into the Chinese army and had to serve as soldiers for at least two years. During this time they received no payment. However, they were supplied with food, weapons and armour.

## FRONTIER GUARD
A battle-hardened soldier keeps guard with his shield and spear. A warrior like this would have kept watch over the precious Silk Road in a distant outpost of the Chinese empire. This model dates from the reign of the Tang emperor Taizong (AD626–649).

*To put on your armour, pull the undergarment over your head. Ask a friend to help with the waist ties. Make holes in the shoulder pads and tie on with string.*

4 Make enough rows to cover fabric. Trim card to fit at neck. Tape rows together. Take armour off fabric and turn over. Attach split pins at all corners.

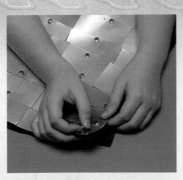

5 Place armour over fabric. Push split pins through top and bottom corners of armour. Pass pins through fabric and fasten. Paint split pins silver.

6 Cut shoulder pads out of thick card. Cut out 5cm squares of silver card to cover pads. Glue to card. Push split pins through. Paint pins silver.

# Festivals and Customs

THE CHINESE FESTIVAL best known around the world today is the New Year or Spring Festival. Its date varies according to the traditional Chinese calendar, which is based on the phases of the moon. The festival is marked by dancers carrying a long dragon through the streets, accompanied by loud, crackling firecrackers to scare away evil spirits. The festival has been celebrated for over 2,000 years and has always been a time for family feasts and village carnivals. The doorways of buildings are traditionally decorated with hand-written poetry on strips of red paper to bring luck and good fortune for the coming year.

Soon after New Year, sweet dumplings made of rice flour are prepared for the Lantern Festival. Paper lanterns are hung out to mirror the first full moon of the year. This festival began during the Tang dynasty (AD618–906). In the eighth month of the year, the autumn full moon is marked by the eating of special moon cakes. Chinese festivals are linked to agricultural seasons. They include celebrations of sowing and harvest, dances, horse races and the eating of specially prepared foods.

**DANCING ANIMALS**
Chinese New Year parades are often headed by a lion (*shown above*) or dragon. These are carried by dancers accompanied by crashing cymbals.
The first month of the Chinese calendar begins on the first full moon between 21 January and 19 February.

**HORSE RACING**
The Mongols, who invaded China in the 1200s, brought with them their love of horses and superb riding skills. Today, children as young as three years old take part in horse-racing festivals in northern China and Mongolia. Archery and wrestling competitions are also regularly held.

## MAKE A LANTERN

*You will need: thick card, pencil, ruler, scissors, compasses, glue and brush, red tissue paper, blue paint, paintbrush, water pot, thin blue and yellow card, wire, tape, bamboo stick, torch, fringing fabric.*

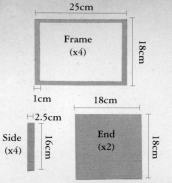

25cm

Frame (x4)

18cm

1cm

2.5cm

18cm

Side (x4)

16cm

End (x2)

18cm

Using the measurements above, draw the 10 pieces on to thick card (pieces not drawn to scale). Cut out pieces with scissors.

1 Using compasses, draw an 8cm diameter circle in the middle of one of the end pieces. Cut out the circle with scissors. Glue on the 4 sides, as shown.

2 Glue together the frame pieces. Then glue the end pieces on to the frame. When dry, cover frame with red tissue paper. Glue one side at a time.

## DRAGON BOATS

In the fifth month of the Chinese year, races are held in the Dragon Boat festival. This is in memory of a famous statesman called Qu Yuan, who drowned himself in 278BC when his advice to his ruler was ignored. Rice dumplings are eaten at the Dragon Boat festival every year in his memory.

## CHINESE LANTERNS

Elaborate paper lanterns brighten up a wedding in the 1800s during the Qing dynasty. Lanterns were also strung up or paraded on poles at other private celebrations and during Chinese festivals.

**3** Paint top of lantern blue. Cut borders out of blue card. Glue to top and bottom of frame. Stick a thin strip of yellow card to bottom border.

**4** Make 2 small holes opposite each other at top of lantern. Pass the ends of a loop of wire through each hole. Bend and tape ends to secure wire.

**5** Make a hook from thick card. Split end opposite hook. Glue and wrap around bamboo stick. Hang lantern by wire loop from hook.

*Light up your lantern by placing a small torch inside it. Decorate with a fringe. Now you can join in Chinese celebrations!*

63

# Ancient Japan

The snowy peak of Mount Fuji, an extinct volcano on the island of Honshu, has been sacred to the Japanese people since earliest times. Legend claims that the first Japanese emperor was Temmu, enthroned in 660BC. History, however, tells us that the empire became a reality about 1,500 years ago. Since then a single royal family has ruled Japan, the world's longest surviving dynasty. This is the story of their empire, of its warlords and farmers and ladies of the royal court. This was the land of the Shinto religion, of *kami no michi* "the Way of the Gods".

# The Land of the Rising Sun

IMAGINE YOU COULD TRAVEL BACK in time 32,000 years. That was when the first settlers reached Japan – a chain of islands between the Asian mainland and the vast Pacific Ocean. On their arrival, the early settlers would have encountered a varied and extreme landscape of rugged cliffs and spectacular volcanoes. Over the centuries, a distinctive Japanese civilization grew up, shaped by this dramatic environment. The Japanese people became experts at surviving in a harsh land. Emperors and shoguns, feuding samurai and peasant workers all played their part in the history of these islands. Many castles, temples, inventions and works of art have survived from the past to tell us what Japanese life was like in ancient times.

**ANCIENT POTTERY**
This decorated clay pot was made by Jomon craftworkers around 3000BC. The Jomon people were some of the earliest inhabitants of Japan. Jomon craftworkers were probably the first in the world to discover how to bake clay in fires to produce tough, long-lasting pots.

**EARLY SETTLERS**
The Ainu people live at the northern tip of Japan. They look unlike most other people in Japan, and speak a different language. Historians believe that they are probably descended from early settlers from Siberia.

## TIMELINE 30,000BC–AD550

From around 30,000BC onwards the Japanese islands have been inhabited. For long periods during its history, Japan was isolated from the outside world. In 1854 that isolation came to an end.

*c.*30,000BC The first inhabitants of Japan arrive, probably across a bridge of dry land, from the continent of Asia.

*c.*20,000BC Sea-levels rise and the Japanese islands are cut off from the rest of the world.

*early pottery*

*c.*10,000BC The JOMON PERIOD begins. The Jomon people are hunter-gatherers who live mainly on the coasts. The world's first pottery is invented in Japan.

*rice fields*

*c.*3000–2000BC People from the Jomon culture move inland. They begin to grow food crops.

*c.*2000–300BC The Jomon people move back towards the coasts and develop new sea-fishing techniques.

*c.*300BC The YAYOI PERIOD begins. Settlers from South-east Asia and Korea arrive in Japan, bringing knowledge of paddy-field rice cultivation, metalwork and cloth-making techniques. Japanese society is transformed from wandering groups of hunters and gatherers. Communities of farmers live together in settled villages.

*Yayoi bell*

30,000BC          10,000BC          500BC          AD300

## DAIMYO AND SAMURAI

A samurai swordsman is shown locked in mortal combat in this woodblock print. Daimyo (noble warlords) and samurai (highly trained warriors) played an important part in the history of Japan. Daimyo controlled large areas of Japan (domains), and served as regional governors. Samurai helped them to keep control of their lands, and fight rival warlords.

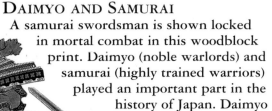

## MAGNIFICENT CASTLES

During the 1500s and 1600s, Japanese craftworkers built many magnificent castles. This one at Matsumoto was completed in 1594–97. Originally, castles were built for defence, but later they became proud status symbols. They were signs of their owners' great power and wealth.

## THE ISLANDS OF JAPAN

The four main islands of Japan stretch across several climate zones, from the cold north-east to the semi-tropical south-west. In the past, each island had its own character. For example, northerners were said to be tough and patient, people from the central region were believed to value glory and honour more than money, while men from the south were regarded as the best fighters.

---

*c.*AD300 KOFUN (Old Tomb) PERIOD begins. A new culture develops. New bronze- and iron-working techniques are invented. Several small kingdoms grow up in different regions of Japan. Rulers of these kingdoms build huge mound-shaped tombs. There are wars between the kingdoms.

*royal tomb*

花剌蟲飛

*Chinese writing*

*c.*AD400 The Chinese method of writing arrives in Japan. It is brought by Buddhist scholars and monks who come from China to work for the emperors of Japan.

*c.*AD500 The YAMATO PERIOD begins. Kings from the Yamato region become powerful. They gradually take control of large areas of Japan by making alliances with local chiefs. The Yamato rulers also claim spiritual power, by descent from the Sun goddess, Amaterasu. Calling themselves emperors, they set up a powerful imperial court, appoint officials and award noble titles.

*Mount Fuji*

AD400                                    AD500                                    AD550

# Eastern Islands

JAPAN IS MADE UP of four main islands – Kyushu, Shikoku, Honshu and Hokkaido – plus almost 4,000 smaller islands around the coast. According to legend, these islands were formed when tears shed by a goddess dropped into the sea. The first settlers arrived on the Japanese islands about 30,000BC and by 10,000BC, a hunter-gatherer civilization, called Jomon, had developed there. At first, the Jomon people lived by the sea and survived by collecting shellfish and hunting animals. Later, they moved inland, where they cultivated garden plots. After 300BC, settlers arrived from Korea, introducing new skills such as rice-growing and iron-working. People began to live in rice-growing villages around AD300 and, in time, groups of these villages came to be controlled by local lords.

Around AD500, the rulers of Yamato in central Japan became stronger than the rulers of the other regions. They claimed the right to rule all of Japan, and to be honoured as emperors. These emperors built new cities, where they lived with their courtiers. However, by 1185 rule of the country had passed to the shogun (a military ruler). There were bitter civil wars when rival warlords fought to become shogun. In 1600, the wars ended when the mighty Tokugawa Ieyasu became shogun. For over 250 years the shogun came from the Tokugawa family. This family controlled Japan until 1868, when Emperor Meiji regained the emperor's ancient ruling power.

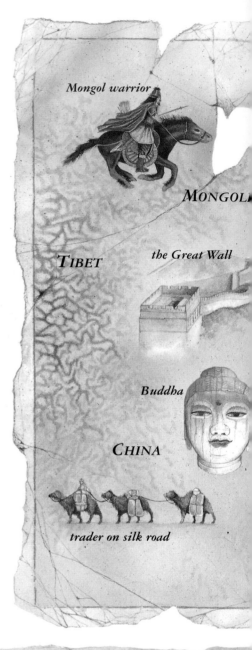

*Mongol warrior*

MONGOL

*the Great Wall*

TIBET

*Buddha*

CHINA

*trader on silk road*

## TIMELINE AD550–1200

AD552 Buddhism arrives in Japan from China and Korea.

AD585–587 Emperor Yomei decides to follow the Buddhist faith. Subsequent emperors also promote Buddhism.

AD646 Emperor Kotoku makes new laws strengthening royal power.

*Buddha*

AD701 Taiho Lawcode brings together many laws, setting up a new system of government. It is strongly influenced by Chinese ideas.

AD710 The NARA PERIOD begins. A new government capital city is built at Nara.

AD712–720 First historical chronicles of Japan, the *Kokiji* (Records of Ancient Matters) and *Nihon Shoki* (Chronicles of Japan) are completed.

AD724–749 Reign of Emperor Shomu.

*palace at Kyoto*

AD794 End of the NARA PERIOD. The HEIAN PERIOD begins.

AD794 Emperor Kammu moves to a new capital at Heian-kyo (modern Kyoto).

c.AD800 The Fujiwara clan of nobles begin to control the government.

c.AD800 Japanese culture replaces Chinese culture at the emperor's court. A new Japanese system of writing is invented.

*Chinese vase*

AD550　　　　　　　　AD650　　　　　　　　AD750　　　　　　　　AD850

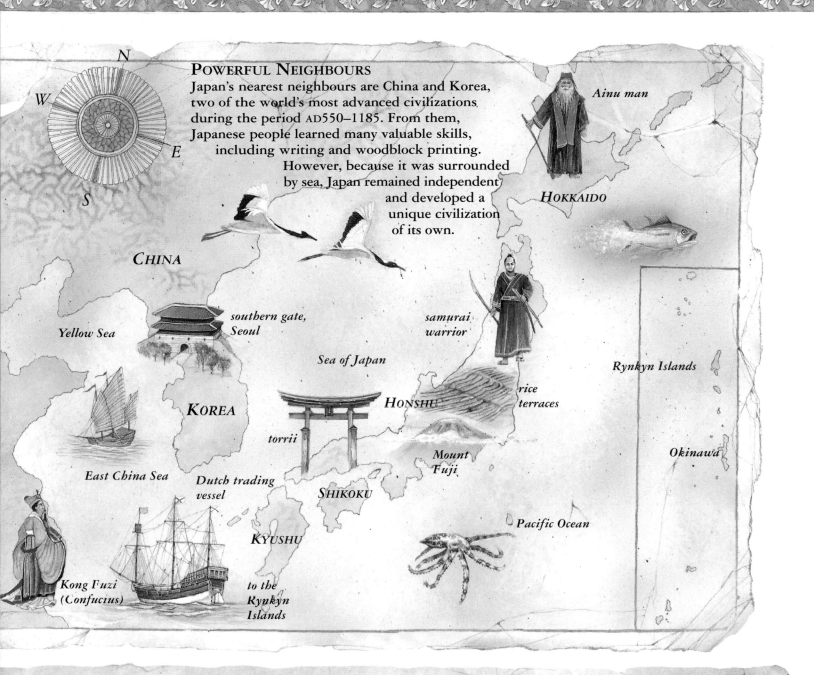

## POWERFUL NEIGHBOURS

Japan's nearest neighbours are China and Korea, two of the world's most advanced civilizations during the period AD550–1185. From them, Japanese people learned many valuable skills, including writing and woodblock printing. However, because it was surrounded by sea, Japan remained independent and developed a unique civilization of its own.

*Ainu man*

N
W
E
S

*Yellow Sea*

CHINA

*southern gate, Seoul*

*samurai warrior*

HOKKAIDO

*Sea of Japan*

*Rynkyn Islands*

KOREA

HONSHU

*rice terraces*

*torrii*

*Mount Fuji*

*Okinawa*

*East China Sea*

*Dutch trading vessel*

SHIKOKU

*Pacific Ocean*

*Kong Fuzi (Confucius)*

KYUSHU

*to the Rynkyn Islands*

---

AD894 Links with China are broken.

*c.*AD900 The invention of new scripts for written Japanese leads to the growth of various kinds of literature. These works include collections of poetry, diaries, notebooks and novels. Many of the finest examples are written by rich, well-educated women at the emperor's court.

*c.*AD965 The birth of Sei Shonagon. Sei Shonagon is a courtier admired for her learning and for her witty and outspoken comments on people, places and events. She writes a famous pillow book (diary).

*c.*AD1000 *The Tale of Genji,* written by Lady Murasaki Shikibu, is completed. This was the story of love, politics and intrigue within the royal court. *The Tale of Genji* is one of the world's first novels. Lady Murasaki was the daughter of a powerful nobleman. She began to write after the death of her husband.

*Lady Murasaki*

AD1159 The Heiji civil war breaks out between two powerful clans, the Taira and the Minamoto. The Taira are victorious.

AD1185 Successive emperors lose control of the regions to warlike nobles. The HEIAN PERIOD ends. The Minamoto family, led by Minamoto Yoritomo, defeat the Taira. They gain control of most of Japan and set up a rival government at Kamakura, far from the imperial capital of Kyoto. Yoritomo takes the title of shogun.

*Minamoto Yoritomo*

AD1000          AD1100          AD1200

# The Powerful and Famous

THE HISTORY OF ANCIENT JAPAN records the deeds of famous heroes, powerful emperors and bold warriors. Men and women who had won respect for their achievements in learning, religion and the arts were also held in high regard. In early Japanese society, royal traditions, honour, skill and bravery in battle were considered to be important, as was devotion to serious study. These principles mattered far more than the accumulation of wealth, or the invention of something new. Business people, no matter how successful, were in the lowest social class. However, during the Tokugawa period (1600–1868) many did gain financial power. Hard-working farmers, though in theory respected, led very difficult lives.

### PRINCE YAMATO
Many stories were told about the daring adventures of this legendary hero. Prince Yamato probably never existed, but he is important because he symbolizes the power of Japan's first emperors. These emperors came from the Yamato region.

### EMPRESS JINGU (ruled c.AD200)
According to Japanese legends, Empress (Kogo) Jingu ruled in about AD200, on behalf of her son. Many legends tell of her magic skills, such as her ability to control the waves and tides.

---

## TIMELINE AD1200–1868

c.AD1200 Trade increases and a new coinage is developed. Zen Buddhism becomes popular during this period, especially with samurai warriors.

AD1274–1281 Mongols attempt to invade, but are driven back by storms.

*samurai warrior*

AD1331–1333 Emperor Godaigo tries to win back royal power. He fails, but his bid leads to a rebellion against the shogun.

AD1336 Ashikaga Takauji takes power and installs Emperor Komyo. He moves his court to Kyoto and encourages art and culture. Links with China are re-opened.

AD1338 Ashikaga Takauji takes the title shogun. The MUROMACHI PERIOD begins.

*samurai swords*

AD1467–1477 The Onin War – a civil war between rival nobles and provincial governors. The shogun's power collapses for a time. This is the first in a series of civil wars lasting until the 1590s. New daimyo (warlords) conquer vast territories in different regions.

AD1540 The first European traders and missionaries arrive in Japan. European traders hope to find spices and rich silks. European missionaries want to spread the Christian faith throughout Japan.

*Portuguese sailor*

AD1200          AD1300          AD1400          AD1500

## TOYOTOMI HIDEYOSHI (1536–1598)

Hideyoshi was a famous war-leader. Along with two other great warlords, Oda Nobunaga and Tokugawa Ieyasu, he helped to unite Japan. The country was unified in 1590, after years of bloody civil war. As a peace measure, Hideyoshi banned everyone except samurai from carrying swords.

## LADY MURASAKI SHIKIBU (c.AD978–1014)

The writer Lady Murasaki spent much of her life at the royal court as an attendant to Empress Akiko. Her book, *The Tale of Genji*, tells the story of the life and loves of Genji, a Japanese prince, in a sensitive and poetic style.

## THE MEIJI EMPEROR (1852–1912)

The Meiji imperial family are shown in this painting. The emperor began his reign in 1867. The following year the shoguns' long period in office was ended when nobles (daimyo) engineered their downfall. The nobles then installed the emperor as a figurehead ruler.

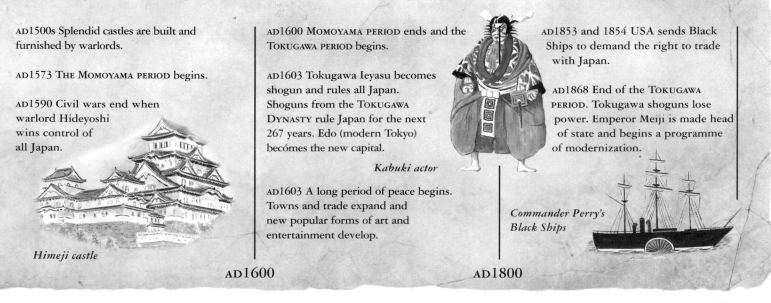

AD1500s Splendid castles are built and furnished by warlords.

AD1573 THE MOMOYAMA PERIOD begins.

AD1590 Civil wars end when warlord Hideyoshi wins control of all Japan.

*Himeji castle*

AD1600 MOMOYAMA PERIOD ends and the TOKUGAWA PERIOD begins.

AD1603 Tokugawa Ieyasu becomes shogun and rules all Japan. Shoguns from the TOKUGAWA DYNASTY rule Japan for the next 267 years. Edo (modern Tokyo) becomes the new capital.

*Kabuki actor*

AD1603 A long period of peace begins. Towns and trade expand and new popular forms of art and entertainment develop.

AD1853 and 1854 USA sends Black Ships to demand the right to trade with Japan.

AD1868 End of the TOKUGAWA PERIOD. Tokugawa shoguns lose power. Emperor Meiji is made head of state and begins a programme of modernization.

*Commander Perry's Black Ships*

AD1600

AD1800

# God-like Emperors

**HANIWA FIGURE**
From around AD300 to AD550, hollow clay figures were placed around the edges of tombs. These figures, shaped like humans or animals, are known as Haniwa.

THE JAPANESE PEOPLE began to live in villages in about 300BC. Over the next 600 years, the richest and most powerful of these villages became the centres of small kingdoms, controlling the surrounding lands. By about AD300, a kingdom based on the Yamato Plain in south-central Japan became bigger and stronger than the rest. It was ruled by chiefs of an *uji* (clan) who claimed to be descended from the Sun goddess. The chiefs of this Sun-clan were not only army commanders – they were priests, governors, law-makers and controllers of their people's treasure and food supply. Over the years, their powers increased. By around AD500, Sun-clan chiefs from Yamato ruled over most of Japan. They claimed power as emperors, and organized lesser chiefs to work for them, giving them noble titles as a reward. Each emperor chose his own successor from within the Sun-clan, and handed over to him the sacred symbols of imperial power – a jewel, a mirror and a sword. Sometimes, if a male successor to the throne was not old enough to rule, an empress would rule as regent in his place.

Descendants of these early emperors still rule Japan today. However, at times they had very little power. Some emperors played an active part in politics, but others spent their time shut away from the outside world. Today, the emperor has only a ceremonial role in the government of Japan.

**NARA**
This shrine is in the ancient city of Nara. Originally called Heijokyo, Nara was founded by Empress Gemmei (ruled AD707–715) as a new capital for her court. The city was planned and built in Chinese style, with streets arranged in a grid pattern. The Imperial Palace was situated at the northern edge.

## FANTASTIC STORIES

Prince Shotoku (AD574–622) was descended from the imperial family and from another powerful clan, the Soga. He never became emperor, but ruled as regent for 30 years on behalf of Empress Suiko. Many fantastic stories were told about him – for example, that he was able to speak as soon as he was born. It was also said that he could see into the future. More accurate reports of his achievements list his introduction of a new calendar, and his reform of government, based on Chinese ideas. He was also a supporter of the new Buddhist faith, introduced from China.

## LARGEST WOODEN STRUCTURE

The Hall of the Great Buddha at Nara was founded on the orders of Emperor Shomu in AD745. The whole temple complex is said to be the largest wooden structure in the world. It houses a bronze statue of the Buddha, 16m tall and weighing 500 tonnes, and was also designed to display the emperor's wealth and power. There is a treasury close to the Hall of the Great Buddha, built in AD756. This housed the belongings of Emperor Shomu and his wife, Empress Komyo. The treasury still contains many rare and valuable items.

## BURIAL MOUNDS

The Yamato emperors were buried in huge, mound-shaped tombs surrounded by lakes. The largest, built for Emperor Nintoku, is 480m long. From above, the tombs have a keyhole-shaped layout. Inside, they contain many buried treasures.

## THE SUN GODDESS

The Sun goddess Amaterasu Omikami is shown emerging from the earth in this print. She was both honoured and feared by Japanese farmers. One of the emperor's tasks was to act as a link between the goddess and his people, asking for her help on their behalf. The goddess's main shrine was at Ise, in central Japan. Some of its buildings were designed to look like grain stores – a reminder of the Sun's power to cause a good or a bad harvest.

# Nobles and Courtiers

I N EARLY JAPAN, everyone from the proudest chief to the poorest peasant owed loyalty to the emperor. However, many nobles ignored the emperor's orders – especially when they were safely out of reach of his court. There were plots and secret schemes as rival nobles struggled to influence the emperor and to seize power for themselves.

Successive emperors passed laws to try to keep their nobles and courtiers under control. The most important new laws were introduced by Prince Shotoku (AD574–622) and Prince Naka no Oe (AD626–671). Prince Naka considered his laws to be so important that he gave them the name Taika (Great Change). The Taika laws created a strong central government, run by a Grand Council of State, and a well-organized network of officials to oversee the 67 provinces.

**BUGAKU**
A Bugaku performer makes a slow, stately movement. Bugaku is an ancient form of dance that was popular at the emperor's court over 1,000 years ago. It is still performed there today.

**POLITE BEHAVIOUR**
A group of ladies watches an archery contest from behind a screen at the edge of a firing range. The behaviour of courtiers was governed by rigid etiquette. Noble ladies had to follow especially strict rules. It was bad-mannered for them to show their faces in public. Whenever men were present, the ladies crouched behind a low curtain or a screen, or hid their faces behind their wide sleeves or their fans. To protect their faces when travelling, they concealed themselves behind curtains or sliding panels fitted to their ox-carts. They also often left one sleeve dangling outside.

**THE SHELL GAME**
*You will need: fresh clams, water bowl, paintbrush, gold paint, white paint, black paint, red paint, green paint, water pot.*

1 Ask an adult to boil the clams. Allow them to cool and then remove the insides. Wash the shells and leave them to dry. When dry, paint the shells gold.

2 Carefully pull each pair of shells apart. Now paint an identical design on to each of a pair of clam shells. Start by painting a white, round face.

3 Add features to the face. In the past, popular pictures, such as scenes from the *Tale of Genji,* were painted on to the shell pairs.

## NOBLES AT COURT

Two nobles are shown here riding a splendid horse. Noblemen at the imperial court spent much of their time on government business. They also practised their riding and fighting skills, took part in court ceremonies, and read and wrote poetry.

## THE IMPERIAL COURT

Life at court was both elegant and refined. The buildings were exquisite and set in beautiful gardens. Paintings based on the writings of courtiers show some of the famous places they enjoyed visiting.

## THE FUJIWARA CLAN

Fujiwara Teika (1162–1241) was a poet and a member of the Fujiwara clan. This influential family gained power at court by arranging the marriages of their daughters to young princes and emperors. Between AD724 and 1900, 54 of the 76 emperors of Japan had mothers who were related to the Fujiwara clan.

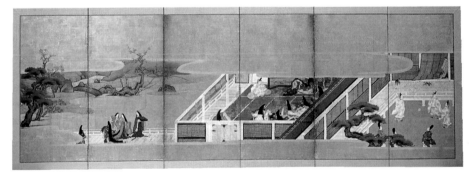

## A LOOK INSIDE

This scroll-painting shows rooms inside the emperor's palace and groups of courtiers strolling in the gardens outside. Indoors, the rooms are divided up by silken blinds and the courtiers sit on mats and cushions.

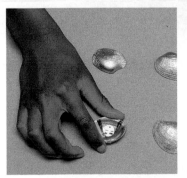

**4** Paint several pairs of clam shells with various designs. Make sure that each pair of shells has an identical picture. Leave the painted shells to dry.

**5** Turn all your shells face down and mix them up well. Turn over one shell then challenge your opponent to pick the matching shell to yours.

**6** If the two shells do not match, turn them over and try again. If they do match, your opponent takes the shells. Take it in turns to challenge each other.

*The person with the most shells wins! Noble ladies at the imperial court enjoyed playing the shell game. This is a simplified version of the game they used to play.*

# Shoguns and Civil Wars

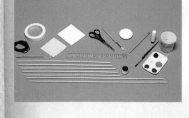

$I$N 1159, a bloody civil war, known as the Heiji War, broke out in Japan between two powerful clans, the Taira and the Minamoto. The Taira were victorious in the Heiji War, and they controlled the government of the country for 26 years. However, the Minamoto rose again and regrouped to defeat the Taira in 1185.

Yoritomo, leader of the Minamoto clan, became the most powerful man in Japan and set up a new headquarters in the city of Kamakura. The emperor continued to act as head of the government in Kyoto, but he was effectively powerless. For almost the next 700 years, until 1868, military commanders such as Yoritomo were the real rulers of Japan. They were known by the title *sei i tai shogun*, an army term meaning Great General Subduing the Barbarians.

### SHOGUN FOR LIFE
Minamoto Yoritomo was the first person to take the title shogun and to hand the title on to his sons. In fact, the title did not stay in the Minamoto family for long because the family line died out in 1219. But new shogun families soon took its place.

### FIRE! FIRE!
This scroll-painting illustrates the end of a siege during the Heiji War. The war was fought between two powerful clans, the Taira and the Minamoto. The rival armies set fire to buildings by shooting burning arrows and so drove the inhabitants out into the open where they could be killed.

### MAKE A KITE

*You will need: A1 card, ruler, pencil, dowelling sticks tapered at each end (5 x 50cm, 2 x 70cm), masking tape, scissors, glue, brush, thread, paintbrush, paints, water pot, paper (52cm x 52cm), string, bamboo stick.*

**1** Draw a square 50cm x 50cm on card with a line down the centre. Lay the dowelling sticks on the square. Glue the sticks to each other and then tape.

**2** When the glue has dried, remove the masking tape. Take the frame off the card. Bind the corners of the frame with the strong thread.

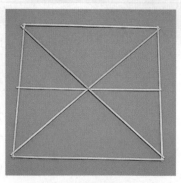

**3** Now position your two longer dowelling sticks so that they cross in the middle of the square. Glue and then bind the corners with the strong thread.

## DYNASTY FOUNDER

Tokugawa Ieyasu (1542-1616) was a noble from eastern Japan. He was one of three powerful warlords who brought long years of civil war to an end and unified Japan. In 1603 he won the battle of Sekigahara and became shogun. His family, the Tokugawa, ruled Japan for the next 267 years.

## RESTING PLACE

This mausoleum (burial chamber) was built at Nikko in north-central Japan. It was created to house the body of the mighty shogun Tokugawa Ieyasu. Three times a year, Ieyasu's descendants travelled to Nikko to pay homage to their great ancestor.

## UNDER ATTACK

Life in Nijo Castle, Kyoto, is shown in great detail on this painted screen. The castle belonged to the Tokugawa family of shoguns. Like emperors, great shoguns built themselves fine castles, which they used as centres of government or as fortresses in times of war. Nijo Castle was one of the finest buildings in Japan. It had "nightingale" floors that creaked loudly when an intruder stepped on them, raising the alarm. The noise was made to sound like a bird call.

*Kites were sometimes used for signalling during times of war. The Japanese have also enjoyed playing with kites for over 1,000 years.*

**4** Paint a colourful kite pattern on to the paper. It is a good idea to tape the edges of the paper down so it does not move around or curl up.

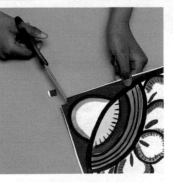

**5** Draw light pencil marks 1cm in from the corners of the paper on all four sides. Carefully cut out the corners of the paper, as shown.

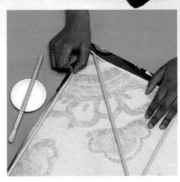

**6** Glue the paper on to the kite frame. You will need to glue along the wooden frame and fold the paper over the edge of the frame. Leave to dry.

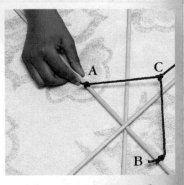

**7** Tie a short length of string across the centre of the kite frame (A to B). Knot a long kite string on to it as shown (C). Wind the string on the bamboo.

# Samurai

**B**ETWEEN 1185 AND 1600 there were a great many wars as rival nobles (known as 'daimyo') fought to become shogun. Some emperors also tried, unsucessfully, to restore imperial rule. During this troubled time in Japanese history, emperors, shoguns and daimyo all relied on armies of well-trained samurai (warriors) to fight their battles. The samurai were men from noble families, and they were skilled at fighting battles. Members of each samurai army were bound together by a solemn oath, sworn to their lord. They stayed loyal from a sense of honour – and because their lord gave them rich rewards. The civil wars ended around 1600, when the Tokugawa dynasty of shoguns came to power. From this time onwards, samurai spent less time fighting. Instead, they served their lords as officials and business managers.

### RIDING OFF TO WAR
Painted in 1772, this samurai general is in full armour. A samurai's horse had to be fast, agile and strong enough to carry the full weight of the samurai, his armour and his weapons.

### TACHI
Swords were a favourite weapon of the samurai. This long sword is called a *tachi*. It was made in the 1500s for ceremonial use by a samurai.

### METAL HELMET
Samurai helmets like this were made from curved metal panels, carefully fitted together, and decorated with elaborate patterns. The jutting peak protected the wearer's face and the nape-guard covered the back of the neck. This helmet dates from around 1380.

### SAMURAI HELMET

*You will need:* thick card, pin, string, felt-tip pen, ruler, scissors, tape measure, newspaper, bowl, water, PVA glue, balloon, petroleum jelly, pencil, modelling clay, bradawl, paper, gold card, paints, brush, water pot, glue brush, masking tape, paper fasteners, 2 x 20cm lengths of cord.

**1** Draw a circle 18cm in diameter on card using the pin, string and felt-tip pen. Using the same method, draw two larger circles 20cm and 50cm.

**2** Draw a line across the centre of the three circles using the ruler and felt-tip pen. Draw tabs in the middle semi-circle. Add two flaps as shown.

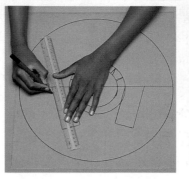

**3** Now cut out the neck protector piece completely, as shown above. Make sure that you cut around the tabs and flaps exactly.

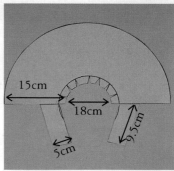

15cm
18cm
9.5cm
5cm

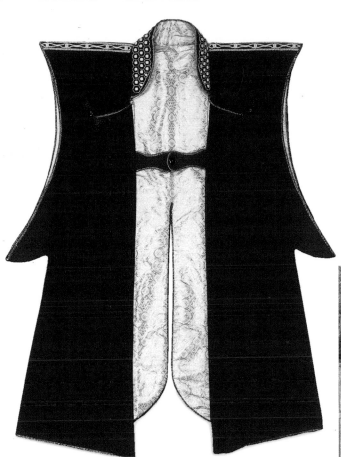

## PROTECTIVE CLOTHING

This fine suit of samurai armour dates from the Tokugawa period (1600–1868). Armour gave the samurai life-saving protection in battle. High-ranking warriors wore suits of plate armour, made of iron panels, laced or riveted together and combined with panels of chain mail or rawhide. Lower-ranking soldiers, called *ashigaru*, wore thinner, lightweight armour, made of small metal plates. A full suit of samurai armour could weigh anything up to 18kg.

## SURCOAT FINERY

For festivals, ceremonies and parades samurai wore surcoats (long, loose tunics) over their armour. Surcoats were made from fine, glossy silks, dyed in rich colours. This example was made during the Tokugawa period (1600–1868). Surcoats were often decorated with family crests. These were originally used to identify soldiers in battle, but later became badges of high rank.

## MAKING BOWS

Japanese craftworkers are busy at work making bows, around 1600. The bow was the Japanese warrior's most ancient weapon. Bows were made of wood and bamboo and fired many different kinds of arrow.

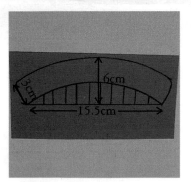

**4** Draw the peak template piece on another piece of card. Follow the measurements shown in the picture. Cut out the peak template.

**5** To make papier-mâché, tear the newspaper into small strips. Fill the bowl with 1 part PVA glue to 3 parts water. Add the newspaper strips.

**6** Blow up the balloon to the size of your head. Cover with petroleum jelly. Build up three papier-mâché layers on the top and sides. Leave to dry between layers.

**7** When dry, pop the balloon and trim. Ask a friend to make a mark on either side of your head.

*Instructions for the helmet continue on the next page...*

79

# The Way of the Warrior

**S**AMURAI were highly-trained warriors who dedicated their lives to fighting for their lords. However, being a samurai involved more than just fighting. The ideal samurai was supposed to follow a strict code of behaviour, governing all aspects of his life. This code was called *bushido* – the way of the warrior. *Bushido* called for skill, self-discipline, bravery, loyalty, honour, honesty, obedience and, at times, self-sacrifice. It taught that it was nobler to die fighting than to run away and survive.

Many samurai warriors followed the religious teachings of Zen, a branch of the Buddhist faith. Zen was introduced into Japan by two monks, Eisai and Dogen, who went to China to study in the 1100s and 1200s and brought Zen practices back with them. Teachers of Zen encouraged their followers to meditate (to free the mind of all thoughts) in order to achieve enlightenment.

### THE TAKEDA FAMILY

The famous daimyo (warlord) Takeda Shingen (1521–1573), fires an arrow using his powerful bow. The influential Takeda family owned estates in Kai province near the city of Edo and kept a large private army of samurai warriors. Takeda Shingen fought a series of wars with his near neighbour, Uesugi Kenshin. However, in 1581, the Takeda were defeated by the army of General Nobunaga.

### SWORDSMEN

It took young samurai many years to master the skill of swordsmanship. They were trained by master swordsmen. The best swords, made of strong, springy steel, were even given their own names.

**8** Place clay under the pencil marks. Make two holes – one above and one below each pencil mark – with a bradawl. Repeat on the other side.

**9** Fold a piece of A4 paper and draw a horn shape on to it following the design shown above. Cut out this shape so that you have an identical pair of horns.

**10** Take a piece of A4 size gold card. Place your paper horns on to the gold card and draw around them. Carefully cut the horns out of the card.

**11** Paint the papier-mâché helmet brown. Paint a weave design on the neck protector and a cream block on each flap. Leave to dry.

## OFF TO WAR

A samurai warrior (on horseback) and foot-soldiers set off for war. Samurai had to command and inspire confidence in others, so it was especially important for them to behave in a brave and honourable way.

## MARTIAL ARTS

Several sports that people enjoy playing today have developed from samurai fighting skills. In aikido, players try to throw their opponent off-balance and topple them to the ground. In kendo, players fight one another with long swords made of split bamboo. They score points by managing to touch their opponent's body, not by cutting or stabbing them!

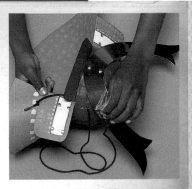

*kendo*     *aikido*

## SURVIVAL SKILLS

Samurai had to know how to survive in wild countryside. Each man carried emergency rations of dried rice. He also used his fighting skills to hunt wild animals for food.

## ZEN

The Buddhist monk Rinzai is shown in this Japanese brush and ink scroll-painting. Rinzai was a famous teacher of Zen ideas. Many pupils, including samurai, travelled to his remote monastery in the mountains to study with him.

*Samurai helmets were often decorated with crests made of lacquered wood or metal. These were mounted on the top of the helmet.*

**12** Bend back the tabs on the peak piece. Position it at the front of the helmet. Stick the tabs to the inside with glue. Hold in place with tape.

**13** Now take the neck protector. Bend back the front flaps and the tabs. Glue the tabs to the helmet, as shown. Leave the helmet to dry.

**14** Stick the horns to the front of the helmet. Use paper fasteners to secure, as shown. Decorate the ear flaps with paper fasteners.

**15** Thread cord through one of the holes made in step 8. Tie a knot in the end. Thread the other end of the cord through the second hole. Repeat on the other side.

# Peasant Farmers

Until the 1900s, most Japanese people lived in the countryside and made a living either by fishing or by farming small plots of land. Japanese farmers grew crops for three different reasons. They grew rice to sell to the samurai or to pay taxes. Barley, millet, wheat and vegetables were used for their own food.

Traditionally, Japanese society was divided into four main classes – samurai, peasant farmers, craftworkers and merchants. Samurai were the most highly respected. Farmers and craftworkers came next because they produced useful goods. Merchants were the lowest rank because they produced nothing themselves.

During the Tokugawa period (1600–1868), society began to change. Towns and cities grew bigger, small industries developed and trade increased. Farmers began to sell their crops to people who had no land of their own. For the first time, some farmers had money to spend on better clothes, houses, and more food.

## WRESTLERS
Sumo wrestling has long been a favourite sport in Japan. It developed from religious rituals and from games held at farmers' festivals in the countryside. Sumo wrestlers are usually very fat. They use their massive weight to overbalance their opponents.

## RICE FARMING
Planting out tiny rice seedlings in shallow, muddy water was tiring, back-breaking work. Rice farming was introduced to Japan soon after 300BC. Most varieties of rice need to grow in flooded fields, called *tanbo* (paddy-fields). To provide extra food, farmers also reared fish in the *tanbo*.

## TERRACING
It was difficult to find enough flat land for growing crops in Japan, so terraces were cut, like steps, into the steep hillsides. Farmland could be shaken by earthquakes or ruined by floods. In years when the harvests failed, there was often famine.

## FAVOURITE FOODS

Soya beans and *daikon* (white radishes) were two popular Japanese foods. The Japanese developed storage methods that would allow them to last for months. The radishes were covered in earth and the beans were dried to provide essential winter food supplies. Farmers grew vegetables like these in small garden plots or in terraced fields.

daikon
*radish*

*soya beans*

## A HARD LIFE

A woman farm-worker carries heavy baskets of grain on a wooden yoke. Although farmers were respected, their lives were often very hard. Until the late 1800s, they had to pay heavy taxes to the emperor or the local lord and were not free to leave their lord's land. They were also forbidden from wearing silk clothes, and drinking tea or *sake* (rice wine).

## THRESHING

Japanese farmers are busy threshing wheat in this photograph taken in the late 1800s. Although this picture is relatively recent, the method of threshing has changed little over the centuries. The workers at the far right and the far left are separating the grains of wheat from the stalks by pulling them through wooden sieves. In the background, one worker carries a huge bundle of wheat stalks, while another stands ready with a rake and a winnowing fan. The fan was used to remove the chaff from the grain by tossing the grain in the air so that the wind blew the chaff away.

# Treasures from the Sea

JAPAN IS A NATION OF ISLANDS, and few people live very far from the sea. From the earliest times, Japanese people relied on the sea for food. Farms, fishing villages and huts for drying fish and seaweed were all built along Japan's rugged coastline. Heaps of oyster shells and fish bones, thrown away by the Jomon people, have survived from over 10,000 years ago.

Japanese men and women took many different kinds of food from the sea. They found crabs, shrimps and limpets in shallow water by the shore, or set sail in small boats to catch deep-sea varieties such as tuna, mackerel, shark, whale and squid. Japanese people also gathered seaweed (which contains important minerals) and other sea creatures such as jellyfish and sea-slugs. Underwater, they found treasures such as pearls and coral which were both highly prized. Specially trained divers, often women, risked their lives by holding their breath for long periods underwater to harvest these precious items. The sea also provided salt, which was collected in salt-pans (hollows built next to the sea). Salt was used to preserve fish and vegetables and to make pickles of many different kinds.

**INSPIRATIONAL**
Strange and beautiful sea creatures inspired Japanese painters and print-makers to create many works of art. This painting shows two flat fish and a collection of shellfish. Tuna, sea bream and salmon were all popular fish caught around the coast of Japan. They were usually grilled or preserved by salting or drying.

**DANGEROUS SEAS**
Japanese sailors and their boat are tossed around by wind and waves in a rough sea. This scene is depicted in a woodblock print by Utagawa Kuniyoshi. The seas around Japan's rocky coasts are often wild and stormy. Being a fisherman was, and still is, a very risky job. Late summer is the most dangerous season to go fishing because monsoon winds from the Pacific Ocean cause very violent typhoon storms. These storms can easily sink a fishing boat.

## SEAFOOD

Sea products have always been very important in Japan. Oysters were collected for their pearls and also for eating. Oyster stew is still a favourite dish in southern Japan. Mussels were cooked to make many tasty dishes. They flourish in the wild, but in Japan today they are also farmed. Seaweed was used to give flavour to foods. Today it is also used as the wrapping for *maki sushi* (rolls of vinegared rice with fish and vegetable fillings).

*oysters*

*seaweed*

*mussel*

## FISHING METHODS

For many centuries, Japanese fishermen used only baited hooks and lines. This limited the number of fish they could catch on any one trip. But after 1600 they began to use nets for fishing, which allowed them to make bigger catches.

## MOTHER-OF-PEARL

Made around 1500, this domed casket is decorated with mother-of-pearl, a beautiful material that forms the coating on the inside of an oyster shell. With great skill and patience, Japanese craftworkers cut out and shaped tiny pieces of mother-of-pearl. These pieces were used to decorate many valuable items.

## OYSTER COLLECTING

Gangs of oyster gatherers collect shellfish from the sea bed. Both men and women are shown working together. Oysters have thick, heavy shells, so the workers have to be fit and strong to carry full buckets back to the shore.

## GATHERING SHELLFISH

Painted in the 1800s, this picture makes shellfish-gathering look like a pleasant task. In fact, hands and feet soon became numb with cold and the salt water made them red and raw.

# Meals and Manners

**J**APANESE FOOD has always been simple but healthy. However, for many centuries famine was a constant fear, especially among the poor. The traditional Japanese diet was based on grains – rice, millet, wheat or barley – boiled, steamed or made into noodles. Many foods were flavoured with soy sauce, made from crushed, fermented soya beans. Another nutritious soya product, *tofu* (beancurd), was made from soya beans softened and pulped in water. The pulp was formed into blocks and left to set. *Tofu* has a texture somewhere between custard and cheese, and a mild taste.

What people ate depended on who they were. Only the wealthy could afford rice, meat (usually poultry) or the finest fish. Poor families lived on what they could grow or catch for themselves.

Until the 1900s, people in Japan did not eat red meat or dairy products. But Japanese farmers grew many fruits, including pears, berries and oranges. One small, sweet orange is named after the Satsuma region in the warm southern lands of Japan.

### FRESH VEGETABLES
A vegetable seller is shown here taking his produce to market. He carries it in big baskets hanging from a yoke supported on his shoulders. This photograph was taken around 1900, but the tradition of going to market every day to sell vegetables started some time around 1600. At this time many more people began to live in towns. The Japanese have always liked their food to be very fresh.

---

### *ONIGIRI* - RICE BALLS

*You will need:* 7 cups Japanese rice, saucepan, wooden spoon, sieve, bowls, 1 tbsp salt, cutting board, 1 tbsp black sesame seeds, ¹/₂ sheet yaki nori *seaweed* (optional), knife, cucumber, serving dish.

**1** Ask an adult to boil the rice. Sieve to drain, but do not rinse. The rice should remain gluey. Place the rice in one bowl and the salt into another one.

**2** Wet the palms of both hands with cold water. Next, put a finger into the bowl of salt and rub a little on to your palms.

**3** Place one eighth of the rice on one hand. Use both hands to shape the rice into a triangle. You should use firm but not heavy pressure.

## SAKE

This *sake* bottle was made almost 600 years ago, in the Bizen pottery style. *Sake* is a sweet rice wine. It was drunk by wealthy noble families and by ordinary people on very special occasions. Traditionally, it was served warm from pottery flasks or bottles such as this one and poured into tiny cups.

## TEA

A servant offers a bowl of tea to a seated samurai. The Japanese believed that no matter how poor or humble people were, it was important to serve food in a gracious way. Good table manners were essential.

## CHOPSTICKS

Japanese people eat using chopsticks. Traditionally, chopsticks were made from bamboo, but today many different materials, including lacquered wood, are used. In the past, rich nobles used silver chopsticks. This was mainly to display their wealth. However, they also believed the silver would help them detect any poison that had been slipped into their food. They thought that on contact with the poison, the silver would turn black.

*ornate chopsticks*

*ordinary chopsticks*

## TABLEWARE

Food was served and eaten in pottery bowls and on plates. In contrast to the round and flat dishes found in many other countries, Japanese craftworkers often created tableware in elegant shapes, such as this six-sided dish.

4 Make more rice balls in the same way. Place each rice ball in one hand and sprinkle sesame seeds over the rice ball with the other.

5 If available, cut a strip of yaki nori seaweed into four and wrap some of your rice balls in it. To serve your *onigiri*, garnish them with sliced cucumber.

*Rice was introduced to Japan in AD100. It has remained the staple food of the islands ever since. Serve your Japanese meal on a pretty dish and eat it with chopsticks.*

# Family Life

FAMILIES IN ANCIENT JAPAN survived by working together in the family business or on the family land. Japanese people believed that the family group was more important than any one individual. Family members were supposed to consider the well-being of the whole family first, before thinking about their own needs and plans. Sometimes, this led to quarrels or disappointments. For example, younger brothers in poor families were often not allowed to marry so that the family land could be handed on, undivided, to the eldest son.

Daughters would leave home to marry if a suitable husband could be found. If not, they also remained single, in their parents' house.

Family responsibility passed down the generations, from father to eldest son. Japanese families respected age and experience because they believed it brought wisdom.

**LOOKING AFTER BABY**
It was women's work to care for young children. This painting shows an elegant young mother from a rich family dressing her son in a *kimono* (a robe with wide sleeves). The family maid holds the belt for the boy's *kimono*, while a pet cat watches nearby.

**WORK**
A little boy uses a simple machine to help winnow rice. (Winnowing separates the edible grains of rice from the outer husks.) Boys and girls from farming families were expected to help with work around the house and farmyard, and in the fields.

**CARP STREAMER**
*You will need: pencil, 2 sheets of A1 paper, felt-tip pen, scissors, paints, paintbrush, water pot, glue, wire, masking tape, string, cane.*

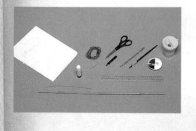

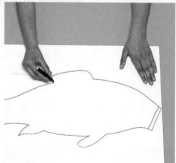

**1** Take the pencil and one piece of paper. Draw a large carp fish shape on to the paper. When you are happy with the shape, go over it in felt-tip pen.

**2** Put the second piece of paper over the first. Draw around the fish shape. Next, draw a border around the second fish and add tabs, as shown.

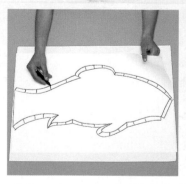

**3** Add scales, eyes, fins and other details to both of the fishes, as shown above. Cut them both out, remembering to snip into the tabs. Paint both fishes.

## PLAYTIME

These young boys have started two tops spinning close to one another. They are waiting to see what will happen when the tops touch. Japanese children had many different toys with which to play. As well as the spinning top, another great favourite was the kite.

## TRADITIONAL MEDICINE

*Kuzu* and ginger are ingredients that have been used for centuries as treatments in traditional Japanese medicine. Most traditional drugs are made from vegetables. The *kuzu* and ginger are mixed together in different ways depending on the symptoms of the patient. For example, there are 20 different mixtures for treating colds. Ginger is generally used when there is no fever.

*kuzu*          *ginger*

## HONOURING ANCESTORS

A mother, father and child make offerings and say their prayers at a small family altar in their house. The lighted candle and paper lantern help guide the spirits to their home. Families honoured their dead ancestors at special festivals. At the festival of Obon, in summer, they greeted family spirits who had returned to earth.

4 Put the two fish shapes together, with the painted sides out. Turn the tabs in and glue the edges of the fish together, except for the tail and the mouth.

5 Use picture or garden wire to make a ring the size of the mouth. Twist the ends together, as shown Then bend them back. Bind the ends with masking tape.

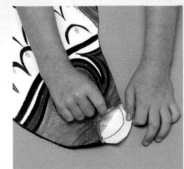

6 Place the ring in the fish's mouth. Glue the ends of the mouth over the ring. Tie one end of some string on to the mouth ring and the other end to a garden cane.

*Families fly carp streamers on Boy's Day (the fifth day of the fifth month) every year. One carp is flown for each son. Carp are symbols of perseverence and strength.*

# Houses and Homes

J APANESE BUILDERS faced many challenges when they designed homes for Japan's harsh environment. They built lightweight, single-storey houses made of straw, paper and wood. These materials would bend and sway in an earthquake. If they did collapse, or were swept away by floods, they would be less likely than a stone building to injure the people inside.

Japanese buildings were designed as a series of box-like rooms. One room was sufficient for the hut of a farming family, but a whole series of rooms could be linked together to form a royal palace. The space within was divided by screens which could be moved around to suit people's needs. Most houses had raised timber floors that were about ½m off the ground.

## LAMPS
This pottery lantern has a delicate, cut-out design and was probably for use outdoors. Inside, Japanese homes were lit by candles. A candle was placed on a stand which had four paper sides. The paper protected the candle from draughts. One side could be lifted to insert and remove the candle. There were many different styles and designs. House-fires, caused by cooking and candles, were a major hazard. They were a particular problem because so many homes were made of wood.

## SILK HOUSE
For many people in Japan, home was also a place of work. Tucked under the thatched roof of this house in Eiyama, central Japan, was an attic where silk producers bred silk-worms.

## MAKE A SCREEN
*You will need: gold paper (44cm x 48cm), scissors, thick card (22cm x 48cm), craft knife, metal ruler, cutting board, glue stick, ruler, pencil, paints, paintbrush, water pots, fabric tape.*

**1** Cut two pieces of gold paper (22cm x 48cm). Use a craft knife to cut out a piece of card the same size. Stick the gold paper to both sides of the card.

**2** Use a ruler and pencil to carefully mark out six equal panels, on one side of the card. Each panel should measure 22cm x 8cm.

**3** Now turn your card over. Paint a traditional picture of Japanese irises, as shown above. When you have finished, leave the paint to dry.

## RICH FURNISHINGS

The interior of a richly furnished building is shown in this print from 1857. Japanese furnishings were often very plain and simple. However, this house has a patterned mat and a carpet on the floor, a tall lampstand, a black and gold side table, and a brightly coloured screen dividing the room. There is also a musical instrument called a *koto* with 13 silk strings.

Wood and paper screens were used to make both outer and inner walls. These could be pushed back to provide peaceful garden views and welcome cool breezes during Japan's hot summers.

## ON THE VERANDA

Japanese buildings often had verandas (open platforms) underneath their wide, overhanging eaves. These could be used for taking fresh air, keeping lookout or enjoying a beautiful view. The people at this inn are relaxing after taking a bath in the natural hot springs.

**4** Turn the screen over, so the plain side is facing you. Using scissors or a craft knife, cut out each panel completely along the lines you have drawn.

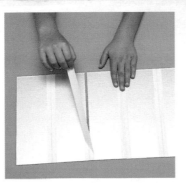

**5** Now use fabric tape to join each of your panels, leaving a small gap between every other panel. The tape will work as hinges for the screen.

*Japanese people liked to decorate their homes with pictures of iris flowers. Traditionally, irises reminded them of absent friends.*

# The Castle Builders

FOR MANY CENTURIES, powerful nobles lived in the city of Heian-kyo (later called Kyoto). But after about AD1000, some noble families began to build up large *shoen* (private estates in the countryside). These families often went to war against each other. They built castles on their lands to protect themselves, their *shoen* and the soldiers in their private armies.

Unlike all other traditional Japanese buildings (except temples), castles were several storeys high. Most were built on naturally well-defended sites such as rocky cliffs. The earliest had a *tenshu* (tall central tower) surrounded by strong wooden fences or stone walls. Later castles were more elaborate buildings, with ramparts, moats and inner and outer courtyards surrounding the central *tenshu*. The period 1570–1690 is often called the Golden Age of castle design when many magnificent castles were built by daimyo (noble warlord) families. These castles were so strong that they challenged the power of the shogun. In 1615, shogun Tokugawa Ieyasu banned noble families from building more than one castle on their estates.

## CASTLE OF THE WHITE HERON

The largest surviving Japanese castle is Himeji Castle, in southern Japan. Some people say it is also the most beautiful. It is often called the Castle of the White Heron because of its graceful roofs, curved like a bird's wings. The castle was built by the Akamatsu family in the 1500s. It was taken over by warlord Toyotomi Hideyoshi in 1580.

## CASTLE OF WOOD

Himeji Castle is made mostly of wood. The building work required 387 tonnes of timber and 75,000 roof tiles. Outside, strong wooden beams are covered with special fireproof plaster. Inside, there are floors and staircases of polished wood.

## CASTLE UNDER SIEGE

The usual way to attack a castle was by siege. Enemy soldiers surrounded it, then waited for the inhabitants to run out of food. Meanwhile, they did all they could to break down the castle's defences by storming the gates and killing the guards.

## RUN FOR IT!

This painted screen shows a siege at Osaka Castle in 1615. The inhabitants of the castle are running for their lives, chased by enemy soldiers. The castle moat and walls are visible in the background.

## IN THE HEART OF THE CAPITAL

Nijo Castle, Kyoto, was begun by warrior Oda Nobunaga in 1569, and finished by Tokugawa Ieyasu. It was designed to give its owner total control over the emperor's capital city – and all Japan.

## SURROUNDED BY WATER

Castles were surrounded by wide, deep moats to keep out invaders. A typical moat might be 20m wide and 6m deep. The only way into the castle was across a wooden drawbridge guarded by soldiers at both ends. The castle was also defended by strong stone ramparts, often 5m thick. They sloped into the moat so that any attacker could easily be seen from above.

## BUILDING MATERIALS

Castles were built of wood such as pine and stone. For the lower walls, huge boulders were cut roughly from the quarries or collected from mountainsides. They were fitted together by hand without mortar so that in an earthquake the boulders could move slightly without the whole building collapsing. Castle stonework was usually left rough, but it was occasionally chiselled to a fine, smooth finish. Upper walls were made of wooden planks and spars, covered with plaster made from crushed stone mixed with water.

*pine*  *limestone*

# Towns and Trade

Until modern times (after around 1900) most Japanese people lived in the countryside. But after 1600, when Japan was at peace, castle-towns in particular grew rapidly. Towns and cities were great centres of craftwork and trade. As one visitor to Kyoto commented in 1691, 'There is hardly a household... where there is not something made or sold.' Trade also increased in small towns and villages, linking even the most remote districts into a countrywide network of buying and selling.

Castle-towns were carefully planned. Roads, gates, walls and water supplies were laid out in an orderly design. Areas of the town were set aside for different groups of people to live and work – nobles, daimyo and high-ranking samurai families, ordinary samurai, craftworkers, merchants and traders. Many towns became centres of entertainment with theatres, puppet plays, dancers, musicians and artists. Big cities also had pleasure districts where the inhabitants could escape from the pressures of everyday life.

### TOWN WOODWORKERS
*Netsuke* were toggles used to attach small items to a *kimono* belt. Three carpenters are carved on this ivory example. Woodworkers were kept busy in towns, building and repairing houses.

### A TRADITIONAL TOWN
This picture was drawn by a visiting European artist in 1882. It shows a narrow, busy street in a Japanese city. Although it is a relatively recent picture, it shows styles of clothes, shops and houses that had existed for several hundred years. The buildings are made of wood and the shops open directly on to the streets. The cloth hangings above the doorways represent the type of shop, for example, knife shop or fan shop. They are printed or woven with *kanji* characters or special designs. The European artist obviously could not read Japanese because the writing on the shop boards and banners is meaningless squiggles.

## SKILLED AT WEAVING SILK

Silk was woven on a loom like the one shown here. This woodblock print dates from about 1770. Towns were great centres of cloth production. Kyoto, in particular, was famous for its silk fabrics patterned with gold and silver flowers.

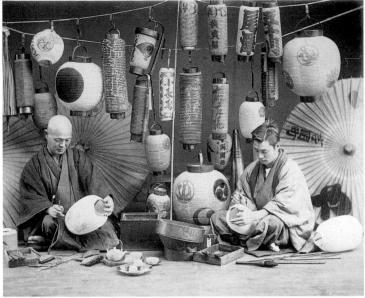

## MANY DIFFERENT CRAFTS

These two men are busy making paper lanterns. From the earliest times craftworkers with many different skills worked in Japanese towns. One list of craft guilds, drawn up in Osaka in 1784, included 24 trades. They ranged from makers of porcelain, parasols and face-powder, to basket-weavers, printers, paper-sellers, paint-mixers, cotton-spinners, ivory carvers, and makers of socks.

## PLEASURE PURSUIT

Actors, musicians and entertainers, like this well-dressed young woman, lived and worked in the pleasure districts of many towns. The most famous was the Yoshiwara district of Edo. In big cities, they were full of inns and restaurants. Young female entertainers were called *geisha*. Merchants and sometimes samurai would enjoy a meal and a drink while the *geisha* danced and sang for their pleasure.

## FIRE HAZARD

Fire was a constant danger in Japanese cities. This was because most buildings were made of wood and packed close together. In an effort to prevent fires from spreading, city rulers gave orders that wooden roof-coverings should be replaced by fireproof clay tiles. They also decreed that tubs of water should be placed in city streets, and watch-towers built to give advance warning of fire.

# Palace Fashions

IN ANCIENT JAPAN, rich noble men and women at the emperor's court wore very different clothes from ordinary peasant farmers. From around AD600 to 1500, Japanese court fashions were based on traditional Chinese styles. Both men and women wore long, flowing robes made of many layers of fine, glossy silk, held in place by a sash and cords. Men also wore wide trousers underneath. Women kept their hair loose and long, whilst men tied their hair into a topknot and wore a tall black hat. Elegance and refinement were the aims of this style.

After about 1500, wealthy samurai families began to choose new styles. Men and women wore *kimono* – long, loose robes. *Kimono* also became popular among wealthy artists, actors and craftworkers. The shoguns passed laws to try to stop ordinary people from wearing elaborate *kimono*, but they proved impossible to enforce.

### PARASOL
Women protected their delicate complexions with sunshades made of oiled paper. The fashion was for pale skin, often heavily powdered, with dark, soft eyebrows.

### GOOD TASTE OR GAUDY?
This woman's outfit dates from the 1700s. Though striking, it would probably have been considered too bold to be in the most refined taste. Men and women took great care in choosing garments that blended well together.

## MAKE A FAN
*You will need: thick card (38cm x 26cm), pencil, ruler, compasses, protractor, felt tip pen (blue), paper (red), scissors, paints, paintbrush, water pot, glue stick.*

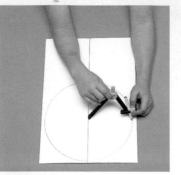

**1** Draw a line down the centre of the piece of card. Place your compasses two-thirds of the way up the line. Draw a circle 23cm in diameter.

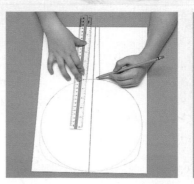

**2** Add squared-off edges at the top of the circle, as shown. Now draw your handle (15cm long). The handle should be directly over the vertical line.

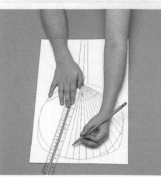

**3** Place a protractor at the top of the handle and draw a semicircle around it. Now mark lines every 2.5 degrees. Draw pencil lines through these marks.

### FEET OFF THE GROUND

To catch insects in a garden by lamplight these women are wearing *geta* (clogs). *Geta* were designed to protect the wearer's feet from mud and rain by raising them about 5–7cm above the ground. They were worn outdoors.

### SILK *KIMONO*

This beautiful silk *kimono* was made in about 1600. Women wore a wide silk sash called an *obi* on top of their *kimono*. Men fastened their *kimono* with a narrow sash.

### PAPER FAN

Folding fans, made of pleated paper, were a Japanese invention. They were carried by both men and women. This one is painted with gold leaf and chrysanthemum flowers.

### BEAUTIFUL HAIR

Traditional palace fashions for men and women are shown in this scene from the imperial palace. The women have long, flowing hair that reaches to their waists – a sign of great beauty in early Japan.

*It was the custom for Japanese noblewomen to hide their faces in court. They used decorated fans such as this one as a screen. Fans were also used to help people keep cool on hot, humid summer days.*

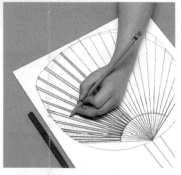

**4** Draw a blue line 1cm to the left of each line you have drawn. Then draw a blue line 2mm to the right of this line. Add a squiggle between sections.

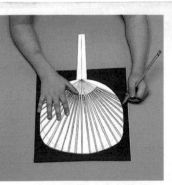

**5** Cut out your card fan. Now use this as a template. Draw around the fan top (not handle) on to your red paper. Cut out the red paper.

**6** Now cut out the in-between sections on your card fan (those marked with a squiggle). Paint the card fan brown on both sides. Leave to dry.

**7** Paint the red paper with white flowers and leave to dry. Paste glue on to one side of the card fan. Stick the undecorated side of the red paper to the fan.

# Working Clothes

**O**RDINARY PEOPLE IN JAPAN could not afford the rich, silk robes worn by emperors, nobles and samurai families. Instead, they wore plain, simple clothes that gave them freedom to move easily as they went about their daily tasks. Men wore baggy jackets and loose trousers, whilst women wore simple, long wrap-over robes.

Ordinary clothes were made from rough, inexpensive fibres, woven at home or purchased in towns. Cotton, hemp and ramie (a plant rather like flax) were all popular. Many other plants were also used to make cloth, including plantain (banana) and the bark of the mulberry tree. From around 1600, clothes were dyed with indigo (a blue dye) and were sometimes woven in complicated *ikat* patterns.

Japan's climate varies from cold and snowy in winter to hot and steamy in summer, so working peoples' clothes had to be adaptable. Usually people added or removed layers of clothing depending on the season. To cope with the rainy summers, they made waterproof clothes from straw. In winter, they wore padded or quilted jackets.

### PROTECTIVE APRONS
These women are making salt from sea water. They are wearing aprons made out of leather or heavy canvas cloth to protect their clothes. The woman on the right has tied back her long hair with a scarf.

### LOOSE AND COMFY
Farmworkers are shown hard at work planting rice seedlings in a flooded paddy-field. They are wearing loose, comfortable clothes – short jackets, baggy trousers tied at the knee and ankle, and shady hats. For working in water, in rice-fields or by the seashore, ordinary men and women often went barefoot.

## MAKE DO AND MEND

Working clothes often got frayed or torn and it was a woman's job to mend them with needle and thread. Women in poor, ordinary families usually made rough, simple clothes for their own families. Sometimes they also bought clothes from travelling pedlars or small shops.

## ARMOURERS AT WORK

Loose, flowing *kimono* were originally worn only by high-ranking families. Before long other wealthy and prestigious people, such as these skilled armour makers, copied them. *Kimono* were elegant and comfortable. However, they were certainly not suitable for active outdoor work.

## FITTING FOOTWEAR

Out of doors, ordinary people wore clogs or simple sandals. The sandals were woven from straw and held on by twisted straw strings. Before entering a house, people always took off their outdoor footwear so as not to bring mud, grass and dirt inside.

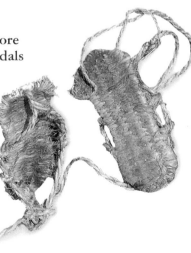

## KEEPING THE RAIN OUT

Cone-shaped hats made of woven straw or bamboo protected people's heads from rain. The sloping shape of these hats helped the rainwater to run off before it had time to soak in. Farmworkers also made rain-capes out of straw matting. In this picture you can see one man bent almost double under his rain-cape (*right*). To protect themselves from the rain, rich people used umbrellas made of oiled cloth.

# The Decorative Arts

THERE IS A LONG TRADITION among Japanese craftworkers of making everyday things as beautiful as possible. Craftworkers also created exquisite items for the wealthiest and most knowledgeable collectors. They used a wide variety of materials – pottery, metal, lacquer, cloth, paper and bamboo. Pottery ranged from plain, simple earthenware to delicate porcelain, painted with brilliantly coloured glazes. Japanese metalworkers produced alloys (mixtures of metals) that were unknown elsewhere in the ancient world. Cloth was woven from many fibres in elaborate designs. Bamboo and other plants from the grass family were woven into elegant *tatami* mats (floor mats) and containers of all different shapes and sizes. Japanese craftworkers also made beautifully decorated *inro* (little boxes, used like purses) which dangled from men's *kimono* sashes.

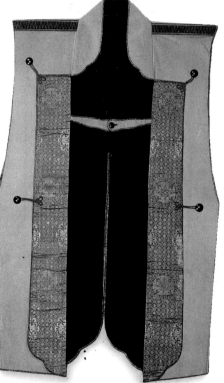

### SHINY LACQUER
This samurai helmet was made for ceremonial use. It is covered in lacquer (varnish) and decorated with a diving dolphin. Producing shiny lacquerware was a slow process. An object was covered with many thin layers of lacquer. Each layer was allowed to dry, then polished, before more lacquer was applied. The lacquer could then be carved.

### SAMURAI SURCOAT
Even the simplest garments were beautifully crafted. This surcoat (loose, sleeveless tunic) was made for a member of the noble Mori family, probably around 1800. Surcoats were worn by samurai on top of their armour.

### MAKE A NETSUKE FOX
*You will need: paper, pencil, ruler, self-drying clay, balsa wood, modelling tool, fine sandpaper, acrylic paint, paintbrush, water pot, darning needle, cord, small box (for an* inro*), scissors, toggle, wide belt.*

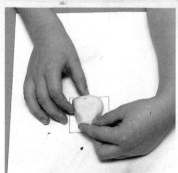

1 Draw a square 5cm by 5cm on a piece of paper. Roll out a ball of clay to the size of the square. Shape the clay so that it comes to a point at one end.

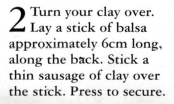

2 Turn your clay over. Lay a stick of balsa approximately 6cm long, along the back. Stick a thin sausage of clay over the stick. Press to secure.

3 Turn the clay over. Cut out two triangles of clay. Join them to the head using the tool. Make indentations to shape them into a fox's ears.

## METALWORK

Craftworkers polish the sharp swords and knives they have made. It took many years of training to become a metalworker. Japanese craftsmen were famous for their fine skills at smelting and handling metals.

## BOXES FOR BELTS

*Inro* were originally designed for storing medicines. The first *inro* were plain and simple, but after about 1700 they were often decorated with exquisite designs. These *inro* have been lacquered (coated with a shiny substance made from the sap of the lacquer tree). Inside, they contain several compartments stacked on top of each other.

## MASTERWORK

This beautiful jar is decorated with a design of white flowers, painted over a shiny red and black glaze. It was painted by the master-craftsman Ogata Kenzan, who lived from 1663 to 1743.

*Wear your* inro *dangling from your belt. In ancient Japan,* inro *were usually worn by men. They were held in place with carved toggles called* netsuke.

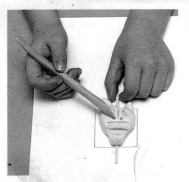

**4** Use the handle of your modelling tool to make your fox's mouth. Carve eyes, nostrils, teeth and a frown line. Use the top of a pencil to make eye holes.

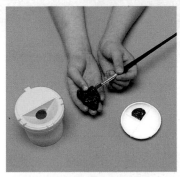

**5** Leave to dry. Gently sand the *netsuke* and remove the balsa wood stick. Paint it with several layers of acrylic paint. Leave in a warm place to dry.

**6** Thread cord through the four corners of a small box with a darning needle. Then thread the cord through a toggle and the *netsuke,* as shown.

**7** Put a wide belt round your waist. Thread the *netsuke* under the belt. It should rest on the top of it. The *inro* (box) should hang down, as shown.

# Wood and Paper

Iᴎ ANCIENT JAPAN, woodworking was an art as well as a craft. Most large Japanese buildings, such as temples and palaces, were decorated with elaborately carved, painted and gilded wooden roofs. Doorways and pillars were also painted or carved. Inside, ceiling-beams and supporting pillars were made from strong tree trunks, floors were laid with polished wooden strips, and sliding screens had finely made wooden frames. A display of woodworking skill in a building demonstrated the owner's wealth and power. However, some smaller wooden buildings were left deliberately plain, allowing the quality of the materials and craftsmanship, and the elegance of the design, to speak for themselves.

Paper was another very important Japanese craft. It was used to make many fine objects – from wall-screens to lanterns, sunshades and even clothes. The choice of the best paper for writing a poem or painting a picture was part of an artist's task. Fine paper also showed off a letter-writer's elegance and good taste.

### WOODEN STATUES
This statue portrays a Buddhist god. It was carved between AD800 and 900. Many Japanese temples contain carvings and statues made from wood.

### SCREENS WITH SCENES
Screens were moveable works of art. This example, made in the 1700s, portrays a scene from Japanese history. It shows Portuguese merchants and missionaries listening to Japanese musicians.

### ORIGAMI BOX

*You will need: a square of origami paper (15cm x 15cm), clean and even folding surface.*

**1** Place your paper on a flat surface. Fold it horizontally across the centre. Next fold it vertically across the centre and unfold.

**2** Carefully fold each corner to the centre point as shown. Unfold each corner crease before starting to make the next one.

**3** Using the creases, fold all the corners back into the centre. Now fold each side 2cm from the edge to make a crease and then unfold.

## GRAND PILLARS

This row of red wooden pillars supports a heavy, ornate roof. It is part of the Meiji Shrine in Tokyo. Red (or cinnabar) was the traditional Japanese colour for shrines and royal palaces.

## HOLY LIGHTS

Lamps made of pleated paper were often hung outside Shinto shrines. They were painted with the names of people who had donated money to the shrines.

## PAPER ART

Paper-making and calligraphy (beautiful writing) were two very important art forms in Japan. This woodcut shows a group of people with everything they need to decorate scrolls and fans— paper, ink, palette, calligraphy brushes and pots of paint.

## USEFUL AND BEAUTIFUL

Trees were admired for their beauty as well as their usefulness. These spring trees were portrayed by the famous Japanese woodblock printer, Hiroshige.

*Japanese people used boxes of all shapes and sizes to store their possessions. What will you keep in your box?*

**4** Carefully unfold two opposite side panels. Your origami box should now look like the structure shown in the picture above.

**5** Following the crease marks you have already made, turn in the side panels to make walls, as shown in the picture. Turn the origami round 90°.

**6** Use your fingers to push the corners of the third side in, as shown. Use the existing crease lines as a guide. Raise the box slightly and fold the wall over.

**7** Next, carefully repeat step 6 to construct the final wall. You could try making another origami box to perfect your technique.

# Writing and Drawing

THE JAPANESE LANGUAGE belongs to a family of languages that includes Finnish, Turkish and Korean. It is totally different from its neighbouring language, Chinese. Yet, for many centuries, Chinese characters were used for reading and writing Japanese. This was because people such as monks, courtiers and the emperor – the only people who could read and write – valued Chinese civilization and ideas.

As the Japanese kingdom grew stronger, and Japanese culture developed, it became clear that a new way of writing Japanese was required. Around AD800, two new *kana* (ways of writing) were invented. Both used picture-symbols developed from *kanji* (Chinese characters) that expressed sounds and were written using a brush and ink on scrolls of paper. One type, called *hiragana*, was used for purely Japanese words; the other, called *katakana*, was used for words from elsewhere.

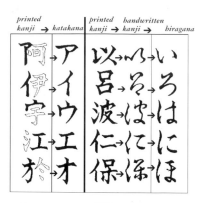

| *printed kanji* → *katakana* | *printed kanji* → *handwritten kanji* → *hiragana* |
|---|---|

## JAPANESE WRITING
Around AD800 two new writing systems, *hiragana* and *katakana,* were invented. For the first time, people could write Japanese exactly as they spoke it. The left-hand side of the chart above shows how a selection of *katakana* symbols developed from the original *kanji*. The right-hand side of the chart shows how *hiragana* symbols evolved, via the handwritten form of *kanji*.

## OFFICIAL RECORDS
This illustrated scroll records the visit of Emperor Go-Mizunoo (ruled 1611–1629) to Shogun Tokugawa Iemitsu. The writing tells us that the palanquin (litter) in the picture carries the empress and gives a list of presents for the shogun.

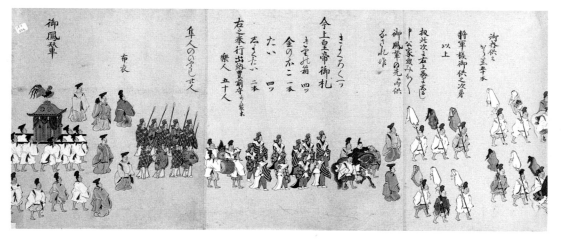

## CALLIGRAPHY

*You will need: paper, ink, a calligraphy brush. (Please note that you can use an ordinary paint brush and black paint if you cannot find a calligraphy brush or any ink.)*

The numbers show the order of the strokes required for this character. Strokes 2, 3 & 4, and 5 & 6, are written in one movement, without lifting the brush.

**1** The first stroke is called *soku*. Begin near the top of the paper, going from left to right. Move the brush sharply towards the bottom left, then lift it off the paper.

**2** Strokes 2, 3 and 4 are called *roku, do* and *yaku*. Write them together in one movement. Apply pressure as you begin each stroke and then release again.

## STORIES ON SCROLLS
Scrolls such as this one were designed to be hand-held, like a book. Words and pictures are side-by-side. Japanese artists often painted buildings with the roofs off, so that readers could see inside.

## PAINTING PICTURES
A young boy is shown here mixing ink for his female companion. The ink is made from compressed charcoal that is dissolved in water to give the ink the required consistency. The artist herself has selected a broad brush to begin her painting.

## PRINTED PICTURES
Woodblock pictures were created by carving an image in reverse on a block of wood, then using it to print many copies of the same scene. Several different woodblocks might be used to print a single picture, one for each separate colour.

*This character is called EI (eternal). It uses all eight major Japanese calligraphy strokes.*

**3** For stroke 5 (*saku*) apply an even amount of pressure as you draw your brush left to right. For 6 (*ryo*), apply pressure at the beginning and release it.

**4** Stroke 7 is called *taku*. Apply even pressure overall to make this short stroke. Make sure that you also make the stroke quite quickly.

**5** Stroke 8 is also called *taku*. Apply an increasing amount of pressure as the brush travels down. Turn the brush back to the right at the last moment, as shown.

# Poems, Letters and Novels

NEW WAYS OF WRITING the Japanese language were invented around AD800. This led to the growth of forms of literature such as diaries, travel writing and poems. Elegant, refined poetry (called *waka*) was very popular at the emperor's court. From about 1600, *haiku* (short poems with 17 syllables) became the favourite form. *Haiku* were written by people from the samurai class, as well as by courtiers.

Women prose writers were especially important in early Japan. The courtier, Sei Shonagon (born around AD965) won praise for her *Pillow Book* – a kind of diary. Women writers were so famous that at least one man pretended to be a woman. The male poet Ki no Tsurayuki wrote *The Tosa Diary* under a woman's name.

**LITERARY LADY**
Lady Chiyo was a courtier and poet in the 1700s. Nobles read and wrote a lot of poetry. It was considered a sign of good breeding to quote from literary works. Letters to and from nobles often contained lines from poems.

**THE WORLD'S FIRST NOVEL**
This scroll shows a scene from the *Tale of Genji*, written in about AD1000 by Lady Murasaki Shikibu. The scroll was painted in the 1700s, but the artist has used a painting style from the period in which the story was written.

**MAKE PAPER**
*You will need: 8 pieces of wood (4 x 33cm and 4 x 28cm), nails, hammer, muslin (35cm x 30cm), staple gun, electrical tape, scissors, torn-up paper, water bowl, masher, washing-up bowl, flower petals, spoon, soft cloths.*

**1** Ask an adult to make two frames. Staple stretched muslin on to one frame. Cover this frame with electrical tape to make the screen, as shown.

**2** Put the frame and screen to one side. Soak paper scraps overnight in water. Mash into a pulp with the potato masher. It should look like porridge.

**3** Half-fill the washing-up bowl with the pulp and cold water. You could add a few flower petals for decoration. Mix well with a spoon.

## POET AND TRAVELLER

The poet Matsuo Basho (1644-1694) is portrayed in this print dating from the 1800s. Basho was famous as a writer of short *haiku* poems. He was also a great traveller, and in this picture he is shown (*right*) talking to two farmers he has met on his travels. Here is a typical example of a *haiku* by Basho:

> The summer grasses —
> All that has survived from
> Brave warriors' dreams.

### JAPANESE PAPER

Japanese craftworkers made many different kinds of beautiful paper. They used tree bark (especially the bark of the mulberry tree) or other plant fibres, which they blended carefully to create different thicknesses and textures of paper. They sometimes sprinkled the paper mixture with mica or gold leaf to produce rich, sparkling effects.

*Japanese paper*

*mulberry bark*

### CRANES ON A CARD

This poem-card contains a traditional *waka* (palace-style) poem, in 31 syllables. It is written in silver and black and decorated with cranes.

*The personality of a Japanese writer was judged by the type of paper they used, as well as by the content of the letter.*

4 Place the screen with the frame on top into the washing up bowl. As the frame and screen enter the water, scoop under the pulpy mixture.

5 Pull the screen out of the pulp, keeping it level. Gently move it from side to side over the bowl to allow a layer of pulp to form. Shake the water off.

6 Take the frame off the screen. Carefully lay the screen face down on a cloth. Mop the back of the screen with a cloth to get rid of the excess water.

7 Peel away the screen. Leave the paper to dry for at least 6 hours. When dry, turn over and gently peel away the cloth to reveal your paper.

# At the Theatre

GOING TO THE THEATRE and listening to music were popular pastimes in ancient Japan. There were several kinds of Japanese drama. They developed from religious dances at temples and shrines, or from slow, stately dances performed at the emperor's court.

Noh is the oldest form of Japanese drama. It developed in the 1300s from rituals and dances that had been performed for centuries before. Noh plays were serious and dignified. The actors performed on a bare stage, with only a backdrop. They chanted or sang their words, accompanied by drums and a flute. Noh performances were traditionally held in the open air, often at a shrine.

Kabuki plays were first seen around 1600. In 1629, the shoguns banned women performers and so male actors took their places. Kabuki plays became very popular in the new, fast-growing towns.

### GRACEFUL PLAYER
This woman entertainer is holding a *shamisen* – a three-stringed instrument, played by plucking the strings. The *shamisen* often formed part of a group, together with a *koto* (zither) and flute.

### POPULAR PUPPETS
Bunraku (puppet plays) originated about 400 years ago, when *shamisen* music, dramatic chanting and hand-held puppets were combined. The puppets were so large and complex that it took three men to move them about on stage.

### NOH THEATRE MASK
*You will need: tape measure, balloon, newspaper, bowl, glue, petroleum jelly, pin, scissors, felt-tip pen, modelling clay, bradawl, paints (red, yellow, black, and white), paintbrush, water pot, cord.*

1 Ask a friend to measure around your head above the ears. Blow up a balloon to fit this measurement. This will be the base for the papier-mâché.

2 Rip up strips of newspaper. Soak in a water and glue mixture (1 part glue to 2 parts water). Cover the balloon with a layer of petroleum jelly.

3 Cover the front and sides of your balloon with a layer of papier-mâché. Leave to dry. Repeat 2 or 3 times. When dry, pop the balloon.

An audience watches a scene from an outdoor performance of a Noh play. Noh drama was always about important and serious topics. Favourite subjects were death and the afterlife, and the plays were often very tragic.

## LOUD AND FAST

Kabuki plays were a complete contrast to Noh. They were fast-moving, loud, flashy and very dramatic. Audiences admired the skills of the actors as much as the cleverness or thoughtfulness of the plots.

## BEHIND THE MASK

This Noh mask represents a warrior's face. Noh drama did not try to be lifelike. The actors all wore masks and moved very slowly using stiff, stylized gestures to express their feelings. Noh plays were all performed by men. Actors playing women's parts wore female clothes and masks.

*Put on your mask and feel like an actor in an ancient Noh play. Imagine that you are wearing his long, swirling robes, too.*

4 Trim the papier-mâché so that it forms a mask shape. Ask a friend to mark where your eyes, nose and mouth are when you hold it to your face.

5 Cut out the face holes with scissors. Put clay beneath the side of the mask at eye level. Use a bradawl to make two holes on each side.

6 Paint the face of a calm young lady from Noh theatre on your mask. Use this picture as your guide. The mask would have been worn by a man.

7 Fit the cord through the holes at each side. Tie one end. Once you have adjusted the mask so that it fits, tie the other end.

109

# Travel and Transport

JAPAN IS A RUGGED and mountainous country. Until the 20th century, the only way to travel through its wild countryside was along narrow, zig-zag paths. These mountain paths and fragile wooden bridges across deep gullies and rushing streams were often swept away by landslides or floods.

During the Heian period, wealthy warriors rode fine horses, while important officials, wealthy women, children and priests travelled in lightweight wood and bamboo carts. These carts were fitted with screens and curtains for privacy and were pulled by oxen. In places where the route was unsuitable for ox-carts, wealthy people were carried shoulder-high on palanquins (lightweight portable boxes or litters). Ordinary people mostly travelled on foot.

During the Tokugawa period (1600–1868) the shoguns encouraged new road building as a way of increasing trade and control. The longest road was the Eastern Sea Road, which ran for 480km between Kyoto and the shogun's capital, Edo. Some people said it was the busiest road in the world.

**BEASTS OF BURDEN**
A weary mother rests with her child and ox during their journey. You can see that the ox is loaded up with heavy bundles. Ordinary people could not afford horses, so they used oxen to carry heavy loads or to pull carts.

**SHOULDER HIGH**
Noblewomen on palanquins (litters) are shown being taken by porters across a deep river. Some of the women have decided to disembark so that they can be carried across the river. Palanquins were used in Japan right up to the Tokugawa period (1600–1868). When making journeys to or from the city of Edo, daimyo and wives were sometimes carried the whole route in palanquins.

## HUGGING THE COASTLINE
Ships sail into harbour at Tempozan, Osaka. Cargo between Edo and Osaka was mostly carried by ships that hugged the coastline. The marks on the sails show the company that owned the ships.

## CARRYING CARGO
Little cargo-boats, such as these at Edobashi in Edo, carried goods along rivers or around the coast. They were driven through the water by men rowing with oars or pushing against the river bed with a long pole.

## STEEP MOUNTAIN PATHS
Travellers on mountain paths hoped to find shelter for the night in villages, temples or monasteries. It could take all day to walk 16km along rough mountain tracks.

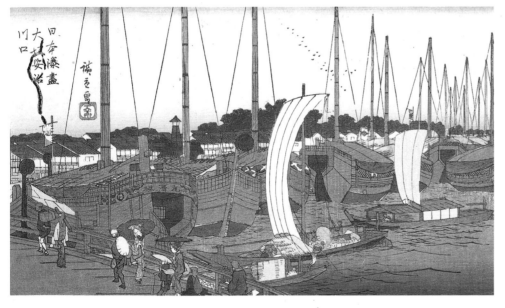

## IN THE HARBOUR
Sea-going sailing ships, laden with cargo, are shown here at anchor in the harbour of Osaka (an important port in south-central Japan). In front of them you can see smaller river-boats with tall sails. Some families both lived and worked on river-boats.

# Remote from the World

**KONG FUZI**
The Chinese thinker and teacher Kong Fuzi (often known as Confucius) lived from 551 to 479BC. His ideas about family life, government and society influenced many later generations in both China and Korea. Chinese scribes took Kong Fuzi's ideas to Japan in about AD552.

**IN WESTERN STYLE**
The young Emperor Meiji took over from the shoguns in 1868. In this picture, leading members of his government meet to discuss foreign policy in 1877. Most of them are wearing Western-style army and navy uniforms.

JAPAN'S GEOGRAPHICAL POSITION has always kept it separate from the rest of the world, but this has not meant total isolation. The Japanese have established links with their nearest neighbours and, sometimes, with lands far away.

In AD588 the first Buddhist temple was built in Japan. Its construction marked the beginning of an era when Chinese religious beliefs, styles in art, clothes and painting, and beliefs about government and society, began to play an important part in Japan. This Chinese-style era ended between AD800 and 900. By that time, Japanese culture had grown strong and confident.

The next important contact with foreigners came when European traders and missionaries arrived in Japan in the 1540s. At first they were tolerated but, between 1635 and 1640, the shoguns banned Christianity altogether and strictly limited the places where foreigners could trade. Europeans had to live within the Dutch trading factory (trading post) on Dejima Island. Chinese merchants were allowed in only a few streets in Nagasaki. This policy of isolationism continued until 1853, when the USA sent gunboats and demands to trade. Reluctantly, the Japanese agreed and, in 1858, they signed a treaty of friendship with America.

## Black Ships

The terrifying Black Ships sailed into Japanese waters in 1853 and 1854. They were members of the United States Navy's squadron of steam-powered paddle-ships under the command of Matthew Perry. Commander Perry's orders were to demand Japanese co-operation with American plans for international trade. Faced with the threat of gunfire, the Japanese government eventually agreed.

## Gardening at Dejima

The land around this house on Dejima Island has been made into a small garden. This island in Nagasaki harbour was the only area where Europeans were allowed to stay during Japan's period of isolation from the world.

## Business in Dejima

This painting from the 1700s portrays European and Japanese merchants and their servants at the Dutch trading factory at Dejima. The artist has shown the merchants discussing business and taking tea in a Japanese-style house furnished with some European-style contents.

## Ideas from Abroad

An American-style steam train travels across Yokohama harbour. This print is from the Meiji era (1868 onwards), the period when Western-style ideas were introduced by the emperor. In the background you can see Yokohama docks which became a major centre of new industries in the late 1800s.

# Gods and Spirits

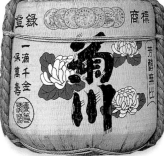

**A**LMOST ALL OF THE Japanese people followed a very ancient religious faith called Shinto. Shinto means the way of the gods. It developed from a central idea that all natural things had a spiritual side. These natural spirits – called *kami* in Japanese – were often kindly, but could be powerful or even dangerous. They needed to be respected and worshipped. Shinto also encouraged ancestor-worship – ancestor spirits could guide, help and warn. Special priests, called shamans, made contact with all these spirits by chanting, fasting, or by falling into a trance.

Shinto spirits were honoured at shrines that were often built close to sites of beauty or power, such as waterfalls or volcanoes. Priests guarded the purity of each shrine, and held rituals to make offerings to the spirits. Each Shinto shrine was entered through a *torii* (large gateway) which marked the start of the sacred space. *Torii* always had the same design – they were based on the ancient perches of birds waiting to be sacrificed.

### AT THE SHRINE
A priest worships by striking a drum at the Grand Shrine at Izu, one of the oldest Shinto shrines in Japan. A festival is held there every August, with processions, offerings and prayers. An *omikoshi* (portable shrine) is carried through the streets, so that the spirits can bring blessings to everyone.

### OFFERINGS TO THE SPIRITS
Worshippers at Shinto shrines leave offerings for the *kami* (spirits) that live there. These offerings are neatly-wrapped barrels of *sake* (rice wine). Today, worshippers also leave little wooden plaques with prayers on them.

### VOTIVE DOLLS

*You will need: self-drying clay, 2 balsa wood sticks (12cm long), ruler, paints, paintbrush, water pot, modelling clay, silver foil, red paper, gold paper, scissors, pencil, glue stick, optional basket and dowelling stick.*

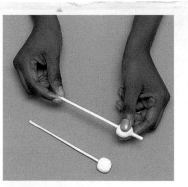

**1** Place a ball of clay on the end of each of the balsa sticks. On one of the sticks, push the clay down so that it is 5mm from the end. This will be the man.

**2** Paint hair and features on the man. Stand it up in modelling clay to dry. Repeat with the woman. Cover the 5mm excess stick on the man's head in foil.

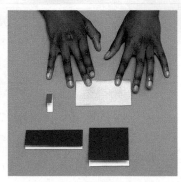

**3** Take two pieces of red paper, 6.5cm x 14cm and 6cm x 10cm. Fold them in half. Take two pieces of gold paper, 10.5cm x 10cm and 1cm x 7cm. Fold in half.

## HOLY VOLCANO
Fuji-San (Mount Fuji) has been honoured as a holy place since the first people arrived in Japan. Until 1867, women were not allowed to set foot on Fuji's holy ground.

## LUCKY GOD
Daikoku is one of seven lucky gods from India, China and Japan that are associated with good fortune. In Japan, he is the special god of farmers, wealth, and of the kitchen. Daikoku is recognized by both Shinto and Buddhist religions.

## FLOATING GATE
This *torii* at Miyajima (Island of Shrines), in southern Japan, is built on the seashore. It appears to float on the water as the tide flows in. Miyajima was sacred to the three daughters of the Sun.

*In some regions of Japan, dolls like these are put on display in baskets every year at Hinamatsuri (Girls' Day), on 3 March.*

**4** Take the folded red paper (6.5cm x 14cm). This is the man's *kimono*. Cut a triangular shape out of the bottom. Cut a neck hole out at the folded end.

**5** Dip the blunt end of the pencil in white paint. Stipple a pattern on to the red paper. Add the central dots using the pencil tip dipped in paint.

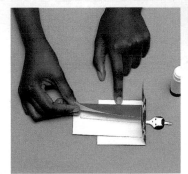

**6** Slip the man's head and body into the red paper *kimono.* Then take the larger piece of gold paper and fold around the stick, as shown. Glue in place.

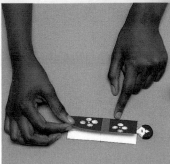

**7** Now stick the gold paper (1cm x 7cm) on to the woman's *kimono*, in the middle. Slip the woman's head and body into the *kimono*. Glue in place.

# Monks and Priests

**MONK AND PUPIL**
A Buddhist sage is pictured with one of his pupils. Thanks to such teachers, Buddhist ideas spread beyond the imperial court to reach ordinary people, and many Buddhist temples and monasteries were built.

AS WELL AS FOLLOWING SHINTO, many Japanese people also practised the Buddhist faith. Prince Siddhartha Gautama, the founder of Buddhism, was born in Nepal around 500BC. He left his home to teach a new religion based on the search for truth and harmony and the ending of all selfish desires. His followers called him the Buddha (the enlightened one). The most devoted Buddhists spent at least part of their life as scholars, priests, monks or nuns.

Buddhist teachings first reached Japan in AD552, brought by monks and scribes from China and Korea. Buddhism encouraged learning and scholarship, and, over the centuries, many different interpretations of the Buddha's teachings developed. Each was taught by dedicated monks or priests and attracted many followers. The Buddhist monk Shinran (1173–1262) urged his followers to place their faith in Amida Buddha (a calm, kindly form of the Buddha). He taught them that Amida Buddha would lead them after death to the Western Paradise. Shinran's rival, Nichiren (1222–1282) claimed that he had been divinely chosen to spread the True Word. This was Nichiren's own interpretation of Buddhism, based on an ancient Buddhist text called the *Lotus Sutra*.

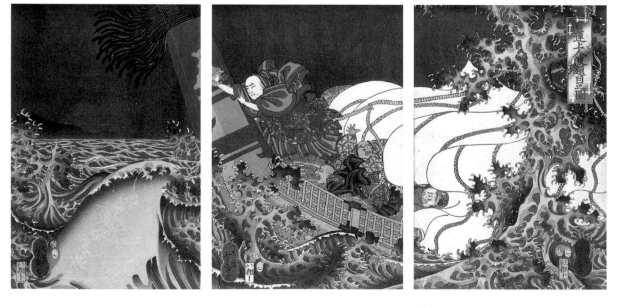

**FAMOUS MONK**
This woodcut of 1857 shows an episode from a story about the Buddhist monk, Nichiren. He was said to have calmed a storm by the power of his prayers. The influence of Nichiren continued long after his death, and many other stories were told about him.

## SCHOLAR MONKS

A group of monks (*left*) study Buddhist scrolls. Monks were among the most important scholars in early Japan. They studied ancient Chinese knowledge and developed new Japanese ideas.

## GREAT BUDDHA

This huge bronze statue of Daibutsu (the Great Buddha) is 11.3m high and weighs 93 tonnes. It was made at Kamakura in 1252 – a time when the city was rich and powerful. The statue shows the Buddha in Amida form – inviting worshippers to the Western Paradise.

## GOD OF MERCY

Standing over 5m high, this statue of Kannon was made around AD700. Kannon is also known as the god of mercy. Orginally Kannon was a man – in fact, one form of the Buddha himself. However, over the years it became the custom to portray him in female shape.

## HOLY FLOWERS

The lotus flower often grows in dirty water and was believed to symbolize the purity of a holy life. It has many associations in literature with Buddhism. Chrysanthemums are often placed on graves or on Buddhist altars in the home. White and yellow flowers are most popular because these colours are associated with death.

*white chrysanthemum*

*yellow chrysanthemums*

*lotus*

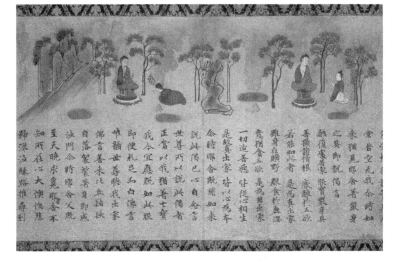

## HOLY WORDS

For many years after Buddhism reached Japan, it was practised mainly by educated, wealthy people. Only they could read the beautiful Buddhist *sutras* (religious texts) like this one, created between AD645 and 794. This sutra was written by hand, but some of the world's first printed documents are Buddhist *sutras* made in Japan.

# Temples and Gardens

Land suitable for growing plants was very precious in Japan, so the people made the best use of it – both for growing food and for giving pleasure. All Japanese people who could afford it liked to surround their homes with beautiful gardens where they could take gentle exercise, read or entertain.

Japanese gardens were often small, but they were carefully planned to create a landscape in miniature. Each rock, pool, temple or gateway was positioned where it could best be admired, but also where it formed part of a balanced, harmonious arrangement. Japanese designers chose plants to create a garden that would look good during all the different seasons of the year. Zen gardens – made of stones, sand and gravel – contained no plants at all.

### PLANTS TO ADMIRE
Artists created and recorded delicate arrangements of blooms and leaves. This scroll-painting of branches, blossom and flowers dates from the 1500s.

### ZEN GARDEN
This is part of a Zen Buddhist garden, made of lumps of rock and carefully-raked gravel. Gardens like this were designed to help people pray and meditate in peaceful surroundings.

### HARMONY IN DESIGN
The Eastern Pagoda at the Yakushiji Temple in Nara is one of the oldest temples in Japan. It was founded in AD680 and the pagoda was built in 730. Pagodas are tall towers, housing statues of Buddha or other religious works of art. Often, they form part of a group of buildings standing in a garden.

### MAKING AN *IKEBANA* ARRANGEMENT

*You will need: vase filled with water, scissors, twig, raffia or string, 2 flowers (with different length stems), a branch of foliage, 2 stems of waxy leaves.*

**1** Cut the twig so that it can be wedged into the neck of the vase. This will provide a structure to build on and to control the position of the flowers.

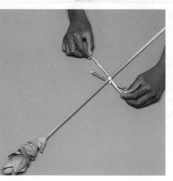

**2** Remove the twig from the vase. Next, using raffia or string, tie the twig tightly on to the longest flower about halfway down the stem.

**3** Place the flower stem in the vase. As you do this, gently slide the twig back into the neck of the vase and wedge it into position as before.

## TREES IN MINIATURE

Bonsai is the Japanese art of producing miniature but fully-formed trees. This is achieved by clipping roots and carefully regulating the water supply. Bonsai originated in China, but became popular in Japan around 1500. A tree that might naturally grow to about 6m could end up just 30cm tall after bonsai treatment. Some bonsai trees are grown to achieve a dramatic slanting or twisted shape.

*bonsai maple*    *bonsai pine*

## CHINESE STYLE

The Tenryuji Temple, Kyoto, stands in one of the oldest Buddhist gardens still surviving in Japan. The garden was created before 1300. It is designed in the Chinese style and made of rocks, gravel, water and evergreen plants.

## GARDENERS AT WORK

A gardener, his wife and son prepare to plant cedar tree saplings. In the foreground, you can see a wooden bucket for watering plants, and a wooden hoe for digging up weeds. At the back, there are nursery beds where seedlings are carefully tended. Cedar trees were, and still are, popular in Japan. The wood is used in the building of houses and the beautiful trees themselves are used to decorate many gardens.

*Ikebana means "living flowers". The three main branches of an arrangement represent heaven, earth and human beings.*

**4** Add the shorter-stemmed flower to the longer stem. Position it so that it slants forwards. Carefully lean it against the twig and the longer stem.

**5** Slip the branch of foliage between the two stems. It should lean out and forward. The foliage should look as though it is a branch growing naturally.

**6** Position some waxy leaves at the neck of the vase. *Ikebana* is the arrangement of anything that grows. Foliage is as important as the flowers.

**7** Add a longer stem of waxy leaves at the back of the vase. This simple arrangement is typical of those Japanese people have in their homes.

# Festivals and Ceremonies

THE JAPANESE PEOPLE CELEBRATED FESTIVALS (*matsuri*) all year round, but especially during the warm months of spring and summer. Many of these festivals had ancient origins and were connected with farming or to the seasons. Others were linked to Shinto beliefs or to imported Buddhist ideas. There were two main kinds of festival. National holidays, such as New Year, were celebrated throughout Japan. Smaller local festivals were often linked to a Buddhist statue or temple, or to an ancient Shinto shrine.

One of the most important ceremonies was the tea ceremony, first held by Buddhist monks between 1300 and 1500. During the ceremony, the host served tea to his or her guests with great delicacy, politeness and precision.

## BOWLS FOR TEA

At a tea ceremony, two types of green tea are served in bowls like these. The bowls are often plainly shaped and simply decorated. According to Zen beliefs, beauty can be found in pure, calm, simple things. Toyotomi Hideyoshi fell out with the tea master Sen no Rikyu over this. Hideyoshi liked tea bowls to be ornate rather than plain.

## LOCAL FESTIVAL

A crowd of people enjoy a festival day. Local festivals usually included processions of portable Shinto shrines through the streets. These were followed by lots of noisy and cheerful people.

## TEA BOWL

*You will need: self-drying clay, cutting board, ruler, modelling tool, cut-out bottom of a plastic bottle (about 10cm in diameter), fine sandpaper, paints, paintbrush, water pot, soft cloth, varnish and brush.*

**1** Roll out a snake of clay 25cm long and 1cm thick. Starting from the centre, curl the clay tightly into a circle with a diameter of 10cm.

**2** Now you have made the base of the bowl, start to build up the sides. Roll out more snakes of clay, 25cm long. Join the pieces by pressing them together.

**3** Sculpt the ridges of the coil bowl together using your fingers and modelling tool. Use the bottom of a plastic bottle for support (see step 4).

## CHERRY BLOSSOM

This woodblock print shows two women dressed in their best *kimonos* strolling along an avenue of flowering cherry trees. The cherry-blossom festival, called Hanami, was a time to meet friends and enjoy an open-air meal in the spring sunshine. Blossoms appeared in late February in the far south, but not until early May in the colder northern lands of Japan.

## BLOSSOM

The Japanese looked forward to the sight of plum blossom emerging, usually in mid February. The plum tree was the first to blossom. In March and April, cherry trees followed suit by producing clouds of delicate pink and white blossom. People hurried to admire the cherry blossom before its fragile beauty faded away. This joyful festival was also tinged with sadness. Spring is the rainy season in Japan and one storm could cause the blossom to fail. The cherry blossom was a reminder that human lives could soon disappear.

*plum blossom*

*cherry blossom*

## TEA CEREMONY

Hostess and guests sit politely on *tatami* (straw mats) for a Zen tea ceremony. This ritual often lasted for up to four hours. Many people in Japan still hold tea ceremonies, as a way of getting away from hectic modern life.

*Design your bowl in a pure, elegant style, like the Zen potters. If you want to add any decoration, make sure that is very simple, too.*

**4** Roll out another coil of clay 19cm long and 1cm wide. Make it into a circle 8cm in diameter. Join the ends. This will form a stand for the bowl.

**5** Turn the bowl over – still using your drinks bottle for support. Join the circular stand to the bottom of the bowl. Mould it on using your fingers.

**6** Leave the bowl to dry. Once dry, remove the plastic bottle and sand the bowl gently. Paint the base colour over it. Leave until it is dry.

**7** Apply your second colour using a cloth. Lightly dapple paint over the bowl to make it appear like a glaze. Varnish the bowl inside and out.

# Glossary

## A

**abacus** A wooden frame with beads on rods, used for calculating.

**acupuncture** The treatment of the body with fine needles, to relieve pain or cure illness.

*aikido* A Japanese martial art in which each contestant tries to overbalance the other.

**Ainu** The original inhabitants of northern Japan.

**alloy** A substance made by mixing two or more metals.

**ancestor** An individual from whom one is descended, such as a great-great-grandfather.

**Anno Domini** (AD) A system used to calculate dates after the supposed year of Christ's birth. Anno Domini dates in this book are prefixed AD up to the year 1000 (e.g. AD521). After 1000, no prefixes are used (e.g. 1912).

**archaeologist** A person who studies ruins and remains.

*ashigaru* A samurai (warrior).

**astronomy** The scientific study of stars, planets and other heavenly bodies. In ancient times it was often mixed up with astrology, the belief that heavenly bodies shape our lives.

## B

**barter** To trade by exchanging goods for others of equal value.

**Before Christ** (BC) A system used to calculate dates before the supposed year of Christ's birth. Dates are calculated in reverse (e.g. 200BC is longer ago than 1BC). Before Christ dates are followed by the letters BC (e.g. 455BC).

**bellows** A mechanism for pumping air into a fire or furnace.

**Buddha** The name (meaning 'the enlightened one') given to Siddhartha Gautama, an Indian prince who lived around 500BC. He taught a new philosophy, based on seeking peace (nirvana).

**Buddhism** A world faith, based on the Buddha's teachings.

**bugaku** An ancient dance form that was popular at the court of the Japanese emperor.

*bunraku* Japanese puppet plays.

*bushido* A strict code of brave, honourable behaviour, which is meant to be followed by the Japanese samurai (warriors).

## C

**character** One of the symbols used in a non-alphabetic script, such as Chinese.

**chopsticks** Short sticks used for eating food in China and Japan.

**civil servant** An official who carries out government administration. Thousands of civil servants worked for the Chinese emperors.

**civilization** A society that makes advances in law, government, the arts and technology.

**clan** A group of people related to each other by ancestry or marriage.

**Confucianism** The Western name for the teachings of philosopher Kong Fuzi (Confucius), calling for social order and respect for one's ancestors.

**cormorant** A coastal and river bird that can be trained to catch fish.

**crossbow** A mechanical bow that fires small arrows or bolts.

## D

*daimyo* In Japanese history, a nobleman or warlord.

**Daoism** A Chinese philosophy based on contemplation of the natural world. It later became a religion with a belief in magic.

**dynasty** 1) Successive generations of a ruling family. 2) A period of rule by emperors of the same royal family. The most important dynasties in the history of the Chinese empire are:

Xia (*c.*2100BC–*c.*1600BC)

Shang (*c.*1600BC–1122BC)

Zhou (1122BC–221BC)

  Western Zhou (1122BC–771BC)

  Eastern Zhou (771BC–221BC)

Qin (221BC–206BC)

Han (206BC–AD220)

Three Kingdoms Period
  (AD220–280)

Jin (AD265–420)

Northern and Southern
  Dynasties (AD420–581)

Sui (AD581–618)

Tang (AD618–906)

Five Kingdoms and Ten
  Dynasties Period
  (AD906–960)

Song (AD960–1279)

Yuan (1279–1368)

Ming (1368–1644)

Qing (1644–1912)

**E**

**escapement** A type of ratchet invented in China, used in clockwork timing mechanisms.

**G**

**garrison** A fort guarded by a troop of soldiers. The word garrison can also refer to the troop of soldiers.

*geta* Japanese wooden clogs or pattens, designed to keep feet dry in wet weather.

**guilds** Groups of skilled workers who checked quality standards, trained young people and looked after old and sick members.

**H**

*haiku* A short poem of 17 syllables, originating in Japan. *Haiku* were popular from the 1600s onwards.

**Haniwa** Clay figures that were buried in ancient Japanese tombs.

**harmony** A pleasing sense of order, based on peace and balance.

**hemp** A fibrous plant, often used to make coarse textiles and clothes.

**I**

*ikat* A weaving technique. The threads are dyed in different colours then woven together to create complicated and beautiful patterns.

*ikebana* A traditional Japanese form of flower arranging.

**imperial** Relating to the rule of an emperor or empress.

*inro* A small, decorated box, worn hanging from the belt in Japan.

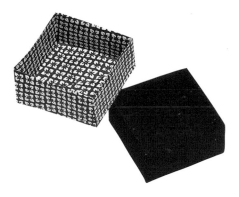

**inscribed** Something that is carved on stone or a similar hard material.

**Islam** The Muslim faith, which proclaims that there is only one God and that his messenger is the prophet Muhammad.

**J**

**jade** A very hard, precious mineral, white or pale green in colour.

**Jomon** An early hunter-gatherer civilization in Japan. It originated in about 10,000BC.

**junk** A large wooden sailing vessel, used in China. It has square sails, stiffened with strips of bamboo.

**K**

**Kabuki** Popular plays performed in Japan from the 1600s.

*kami* The sacred spirits of Japanese religious tradition.

*kana* The name for the Japanese method of writing.

*kanji* The characters used for writing Japanese before about AD800.

**kaolin** A fine white clay used in porcelain and paper-making.

*kendo* A Japanese martial art in which contestants fight each other with bamboo swords.

*kimono* A Japanese loose robe with wide sleeves, worn by men and women.

**kitchen god** A god whose picture was kept in Chinese kitchens, to bring good luck to the home.

*kuzu* A plant with a fleshy root that is dried and used in traditional Japanese medicine.

## L

**lacquer** A thick, coloured varnish used to coat wood, metal or leather.

**litter** A portable bed.

**lodestone** A type of magnetic iron ore, also called magnetite.

**loom** A frame or machine used for weaving cloth.

**lotus** A type of water lily.

**lychee** A soft Chinese fruit.

## M

**magistrate** In imperial China, an officer of justice, similar to a local judge.

**martial arts** A mixture of spiritual discipline and battle training. Japanese martial arts include kendo and aikido. Chinese martial arts include kung fu (*gongfu*), swordplay (*jianwu*) and the gentler tai chi (*taijiquan*).

**mica** A flaky, shiny metal.

**millet** A type of grain crop.

**mint** To make metal coins (or the place where this takes place).

**monsoon** Seasonal winds that blow in southern Asia, bringing heavy rain.

**mosaics** Tiny pieces of colourful stone, shell or glass that are used to make pictures or to decorate objects.

**myth** Any ancient tale or legend that describes gods, spirits or fantastic creatures.

## N

**nape** The back of the neck.

*netsuke* Small toggles, carved from ivory and used to attach items to belts.

**Noh** A dignified, very stylized drama that originated in Japan about 700 years ago.

## O

*obi* A wide sash, part of the traditional costume dress for Japanese women.

*omikoshi* A portable shrine used in Japan.

## P

**pagoda** A traditional form of Buddhist architecture, found in China and Japan. It is made up of a multi-storey tower and is often used as a temple.

**peasant** A poor country dweller, someone who works the land.

**pillow book** A collection of short notes and writings, like a diary.

**Pinyin** The modern method for converting Chinese characters into the Roman (Western) alphabet.

**plate-armour** Protective clothing made of overlapping plates of metal.

**porcelain** The finest quality of pottery. It is made with kaolin and baked at a high temperature.

**province** Part of the empire that has been marked off for administrative purposes.

## R

**regent** Someone who rules a country on behalf of another person.

## S

*sake* A Japanese rice wine.

**sampan** A small Chinese wooden boat, with a cabin made of matting.

**samurai** The knights of medieval Japan. After 1192 they were awarded land in return for serving their lord, or *daimyo*.

**scroll-painting** A painting on a long roll of paper.

**sericulture** The breeding of silk worms in order to make yarn.

**Shinto** An ancient Japanese religion, known as the "way of the gods", based on honouring holy spirits.

**shogun** A military commander in Japan. Shoguns effectively ruled the country from 1185–1868.

**shrine** A sacred place used for religious worship.

**silkworm** The larva (caterpillar) of a silkmoth.

**smelt** To extract a metal from its ore by heating it in a furnace.

**sumo** A type of wrestling popular in Japan.

## T

*tanbo* Flooded fields where rice was grown.

*tatami* A reed mat used as floor covering in Japanese homes.

**terracotta** A composite of baked clay and sand used to make statues, figurines and pottery.

**textile** Any cloth woven from fibres, such as silk or cotton.

**threshing** Separating grains of wheat or rice from their stalks.

**tofu** (Chinese, doufu) Bean curd – a nourishing food made from pulped soy beans, used in both Japanese and Chinese cooking.

**tomb** A vault in which dead bodies are placed. In imperial China, the tombs of emperors and noblemen were often filled with beautiful objects of great value.

*torii* The traditional gateway to a Shinto shrine.

## U

*uji* A Japanese clan.

## W

*waka* Elegant poetry, popular at the emperor's court.

**ward** A walled district, one of many built within the outer walls of cities in imperial China.

**warlord** A man who keeps a private army and controls a large region of a country by force.

**winnowing** Separating grains of wheat or rice from husks.

**wisteria** A Chinese climbing shrub, with blue flowers.

## X

**xiang qi** A traditional Chinese boardgame, similar to chess.

## Y

**yak** A long-haired ox, herded on the Tibetan plateau and Himalayan mountains of China.

**yin and yang** The traditional belief of Daoism that two life forces must be balanced to achieve harmony. Yin is negative, feminine and dark, while yang is positive, masculine and light.

**yoke** A long piece of wood or bamboo, placed over the shoulders to help carry heavy loads.

## Z

**Zen** A branch of the Buddhist faith that was popular among the samurai.

# Index

## A

abacus 34–5
acupuncture 34
Ainu people 66, 69
Amida Buddha 116
armour 60–1, 78–9
astronomy 34, 39

## B

bamboo 24, 30, 48, 50,
  55, 56, 58
Beijing 11, 14, 15, 16, 17,
  22, 36, 40, 41
bonsai 119
bows and arrows 79, 80
Boxer Rebellion 15
bronze 10, 31, 40–1, 46
Buddhism 12, 13, 18–19,
  22–3, 40, 48, 51, 67, 68,
  70, 73, 80–1, 102, 112,
  116–18, 120–1
bugaku 74
bunraku 108
bushido 80

## C

calendar 12, 62
calligraphy 50–1, 103–5
carp streamer 88–9
castles 67, 71, 77, 92–3, 94
Chang Jiang (Yangzi
  River) 12, 13, 56, 58
Chang'an (Xian) 10, 11,
  19, 23, 32, 33, 56
children 88–9, 105
China 68, 69, 70, 112
Christianity 18
civil service 20, 21, 26, 47
climate 67, 98, 99
cloth and clothes 66, 79,
  88, 94–102

Confucianism 11, 14, 18, 26
Confucius see Kong Fuzi
cosmetics 96
courtiers 74–5, 96–7, 106

## D

daimyo 67, 70–1, 78–80,
  92–3, 94
dance 94–5
Daoism 11, 12, 14, 18, 34,
  48, 54
Dejima Island 112–13
dolls 114–15
dragons 25, 40, 45, 46,
  48, 62
dynasties 16

## E

earthquakes 38, 39, 90
Edo 71, 110
education 20, 21, 26
emperors 10, 14–17, 46,
  66, 67, 68–71, 72–3, 74,
  75, 78
engineering 36–7, 56
examinations 20, 21
exploration 14–15, 58–9

## F

family life 26–7, 88–9
fans 96–7
farming 10, 20, 21, 28–9,
  31, 66, 68, 70, 71, 73,
  82–3, 86, 88, 98–9
festivals 62–3, 89, 120–1
fingernails 41, 46
fish and shellfish 66, 82,
  84–5
flowers 117, 118–19, 121
food 82–7
foot binding 26

Forbidden City 16, 17,
  40–1
foreigners, contact with
  66, 69, 70, 71, 112–13
Fuji, Mount 67, 69, 115
Fujiwara clan 68, 75

## G

gambling 54–5
games and pastimes 54–5
gardens 24–5, 118–19
geishas 95
Gemmei, Empress 72
Genghis Khan 14
geta 97
Godaigo, Emperor 70
Go-Mizunoo, Emperor 104
Grand Canal 11, 12, 13,
  14, 36–7
Great Wall 11, 12, 13,
  36–7, 61
Guangzhou (Canton) 23
gunpowder 38

## H

haiku 106–7
hairstyles 96–7, 98
Han dynasty 11, 12, 15,
  24, 26, 40
Han Gaozu (Liu Bang) 11, 15
Haniwa figures 72
Heian period 68, 69, 110
Heian-kyo 68
Heiji civil war 69, 76
helmets 78–81, 100
Hideyoshi, Toyotomi 71,
  92, 120
Himeji Castle 71, 92
Hiroshige 103
Hokkaido 67, 68, 69
Hong Kong 15

Honshu 67, 68, 69
horses 49, 55, 56–7, 60, 62
housing 90–1
Huang He (Yellow River)
  12, 13, 58
hunting 10, 54

## I

ikebana 118–19
inro 100–1
inventions 21, 28, 32,
  34–5, 38–9
iron 11, 28, 40–1, 56
Islam 13, 18, 19
islands 67, 68–9, 84
Izu 114

## J

jade 11, 46, 60
jewellery 40–1, 46–7
Jingu, Empress 70
Jomon people 66, 68, 84
junks 58–9

## K

kabuki theatre 71, 108–9
Kaifeng 33
Kamakura 69, 76
Kammu, Emperor 68
kanji 94, 104–5
Kannon 117
Ki no Tsurayuki 106
kimono 88, 94, 96–7,
  100, 121
kites 54–55, 76–7, 89
Kofun (Old Tomb) period 67
Kokiji 68
Komyo, Emperor 70
Kong Fuzi (Confucius) 11,
  14, 18, 20, 21, 26, 60,
  69, 112

Korea 69
Kotoku, Emperor 68
Kublai Khan 14, 15
kung fu 54
*kuzu* 89
Kyoto 68, 69, 76, 92–3, 94, 95, 110, 119
Kyushu 67, 68. 69

**L**
lacquer 42–3, 60, 100–1
lamps and lanterns 62–3
Laozi 11, 14
Li Bai 13
Li Sixun 48
Li Zicheng 15
literature 69, 71, 106–7
litters 17, 56, 57
Liu Sheng 11
Liu Xiu 12
locks and keys 38
Longshan culture 10

**M**
Manchus 12, 15, 46
martial arts 54, 81
medicine 34–5, 89
Meiji, Emperor 68, 71, 112, 113
merchants 20, 21, 32–3, 42, 46
metal working 10, 11, 40–1, 66–68, 78–9, 100–1, 117
Minamoto Yoritomo 69, 76
Ming dynasty 12, 13, 14, 15, 43, 48, 49, 54
Momoyama period 71
money 14, 21, 32
Mongols 12, 14–15, 36, 62, 68, 70

monks 111, 116–17
Murasaki Shikibu, Lady 69, 71, 106
Muromachi period 70
music 52–3, 91, 94–5, 108–9

**N**
Nanjing, Treaty of 15
Nara 68, 72, 73, 118
*netsuke* 94, 100–1
New Year 30, 33, 62
Nijo Castle 77, 93
Nikko 77
Nintoku, Emperor 73
Nobunaga, Oda 71, 80, 93
Noh theatre 108–9

**O**
*obi* 97
Okinawa Islands 69
*onigiri* 86–7
Onin War 70
Opium Wars 15
*origami* 102–3

**P**
paddy-fields 66, 82, 98
pagodas 22–3, 118
painting 26, 48–9, 75–77, 79, 81, 84, 102, 105, 118
palaces 10, 16, 17, 22
palanquins 104, 110
paper 90, 91, 95, 96–7, 100, 102–3, 106–7
parasols 95, 96
peasants 20–1, 37
Perry, Commander Matthew 71, 113
pigtails 46
plays and operas 52–3

poetry 12, 13, 50, 52
Polo, Marco 14, 15, 37
porcelain 32, 42–3, 49
pottery 10, 21, 28, 42–3, 66, 68, 72, 87, 90, 95, 100–1, 120–1
printing 13, 14, 38–9, 48, 50–1, 69, 84, 91, 103, 105, 116–17
puppets 52
Puyi 15

**Q**
Qin dynasty 15
Qin Shi Huangdi (Zheng) 10, 11, 15, 17, 32
Qing dynasty 15, 16, 17, 21, 43, 46, 54

**R**
Red Turban Rebellion 14
religion 11, 12, 13, 14, 16, 18–19, 30, 67, 68, 70, 72, 73, 80–1, 89, 102, 103, 114–17, 120
Republic of China 12, 15
rice 21, 28–31, 66, 68, 69, 81, 82–3, 86–7, 98

**S**
*sake* 83, 87, 114
sampans 58–9
samurai 66, 67, 69, 70, 71, 78–81, 82, 87, 94–6, 100
science 34–5, 38–9
screens 90–1, 93, 102
Sei Shonagon 69, 106
Shang dynasty 10, 16, 22, 30, 31, 40
Shikoku 67, 68, 69
Shinto 103, 114–15, 120

ships 38, 44, 58–9
shoguns 66, 68, 69, 71, 76–7, 104, 110
Shomu, Emperor 68, 73
Shotoku, Prince 73, 74
silk 10, 21, 32, 38, 44–5, 46, 47, 48, 90, 95, 97
Silk Road 11, 13, 32–3, 56–7, 61
smelting 40–1
Song dynasty 14, 26, 33
Stone Age 10
Sui dynasty 12, 36
sumo wrestling 82
swords 70, 78, 80, 101

**T**
*tachi* 78
tai chi 54
Taika Laws 74
Taira clan 69, 76
*Tale of Genji* 69, 71, 106
Tang dynasty 12, 28, 30, 32, 33, 47, 48, 60
tea 21, 28, 32, 87, 120–1
temples 10, 11, 13, 16, 19, 22, 25, 72–73, 89, 102–3, 111, 114–15, 118–19
terracotta army 10, 11
theatre 71, 94, 108–9
Tibet 12, 17, 23
Tokugawa Ieyasu 68, 71, 77, 92, 93, 104
Tokugawa period 70, 71, 77, 78–9, 82, 110
Tokyo 71, 103
tombs 10, 11, 43, 49, 67, 72, 73, 77
tools 21, 28, 40
*torii* 69, 114–15
towns 94–5

trade 11, 12, 13, 20, 21, 23, 32–9, 42–3, 56–9, 68–9, 70, 71, 94–5, 99, 111–13
transport 17, 36–7, 44, 56–9, 104, 110

**V**
volcanoes 66, 114–15

**W**
*waka* 106–7
weapons 40, 54, 60–1
weddings 26, 63
Western powers 15, 17, 23, 61
women 14–15, 30, 44, 47, 55, 69, 88–9, 95, 96–9, 106, 115
woodworking 73, 90–1, 92, 94, 102–3, 119
writing 26, 50–1, 67, 68, 69, 94, 103–7
Wu Zetian 13, 15, 41

**X**
Xia dynasty 10, 16

**Y**
Yamato period 67, 68, 72–3
Yangshao culture 10
Yayoi period 66
Yellow Turban Rebellion 12
yin and yang 18
Yuan dynasty 14

**Z**
Zen Buddhism 70, 80–1, 119, 120–1
Zhang Heng 38, 39
Zheng He 14–15, 58–9
Zhou dynasty 10, 11, 16

HPL